Graceful Living

Graceful LIVING

*Meditations to Help You Grow
Closer to God Day by Day*

JOHNNETTE S. BENKOVIC

EWTN PUBLISHING, INC.
Irondale, Alabama

EWTN Publishing, Inc.
5817 Old Leeds Road, Irondale, AL 35210
Distributed by Sophia Institute Press, Box 5284, Manchester, NH 03108

Library of Congress Cataloging-in-Publication Data

Names: Benkovic, Johnnette S., author.
Title: Graceful living : meditations to help you grow closer to God day by
   day / Johnnette S. Benkovic.
Description: Irondale, Alabama : EWTN Publishing, Inc., 2016.
Identifiers: LCCN 2016033290 ISBN 9781682780206 (hardcover : alk. paper)
Subjects: LCSH: Devotional calendars—Catholic Church.
Classification: LCC BX2170.C56 B46 2016 DDC 242/.2—dc23 LC record available at https://lccn.loc.gov/2016033290

To my granddaughters,
Julia, Carmen, Josephine, and Baby Parsons.

May you seek purity of heart, generosity of spirit,

and authenticity of life in all things,

for the glory and honor of God!

Grammy loves you!

Contents

Graceful Living

INTRODUCTION

Through the years, the saints have been my faithful friends. Their holy witness has inspired me, encouraged me, and strengthened me in my difficult moments as well as my joyful ones. At every turn, my elder brothers and sisters in Christ have accompanied me on my journey to union with God. For this reason I am happy to offer you *Graceful Living*, a collection of quotations from Scripture, the saints, and other holy men and women, with questions for reflection. Additionally, you will discover biographies of saints and a collection of stories from my own daily life scattered through these pages. My prayer is that this book will help you enter into an ever-deepening experience of God.

May I suggest some steps to help you maximize your use of *Graceful Living*? They can help you to dig deeply into the spiritual and practical wisdom of the Church gathered here.

- *Use* Graceful Living *in your time of prayer.* An ancient form of prayer is *Lectio Divina,* which simply means "holy reading." It is a prayerful endeavor to mine the gems contained for us in the material we read. This means our goal is not to "get through" the content, but to have the content "get through" us.

- *Say a prayer to the Holy Spirit before you begin.* Ask Him to help you become recollected so your time of prayer is fruitful, making manifest the grace God would have you receive.

- *Read each quotation slowly.* Ponder it in your heart. Let the mystery it contains awaken and unfold within you. Note and linger over any words, phrases, or ideas that move you in some way. Is there a memory sparked? An insight or new understanding given? An instruction offered? What might God be saying to you through it? Stay with it until you feel the "movement" is completed. This is the action of grace.

- *Review the questions for reflection.* They are "prompters" meant to help you dig into the quotation to "hear" the word God has for you in it. I urge you to keep a journal so you can record your insights, thoughts, and illuminations. This solidifies the grace and provides you with a record of your "salvation journey." It also enables you to see God's transforming presence in your life.

- *Respond to God's action within you through a prayer.* In the language of the spiritual life, this is called a "colloquy." This should be a prayer of the heart. It is, in a way, your *fiat*—your "let it be done unto me." It may be a prayer of thanksgiving, a prayer of repentance, or a prayer for wisdom and guidance. It may also be a deep interior cry asking God for His healing love and mercy. Know that God hears you with a ready and loving ear.

What joy would be mine if *Graceful Living* became a life-changing experience for you! *Prosit!*

With hope-filled expectation,

Johnnette Benkovic
July 11, 2016
Feast of St. Benedict, Abbot

Chapter One

Meditations

FOR

JANUARY

January 1

SOLEMNITY OF THE BLESSED VIRGIN MARY, THE MOTHER OF GOD

Mary, Mother of God, we salute you. Precious vessel, worthy of the whole world's reverence, you are an ever-shining light, the crown of virginity, the symbol of orthodoxy, an indestructible temple, the place that held him whom no place can contain, mother and virgin. Because of you the holy gospels could say: Blessed is he who comes in the name of the Lord.

—Saint Cyril of Alexandria, *Catechetical Lectures*

This quote contains several descriptions of the Blessed Virgin Mary. What are they? How does each aptly apply to her?

January 2

I want to be completely transformed into your mercy and to be your living reflection, O Lord. May the greatest of all divine attributes, that of your unfathomable mercy, pass through my heart and soul to my neighbor.

—From a prayer of St. Faustina Kowalska

In whose life would the Lord ask me today to be a conduit of His love and mercy? From whom would I most like to withhold love and mercy? In what practical way can I respond in love to others, especially those whom I find most difficult to love?

January 3

For to us a child is born,
to us a son is given;
and the government will be upon his shoulder,
and his name will be called
"Wonderful Counselor, Mighty God,
Everlasting Father, Prince of Peace."

—Isaiah 9:6

In what specific experiences or circumstances in my life have I experienced Jesus as "Wonderful Counselor"? "Mighty God"? "Everlasting Father"? "Prince of Peace"? I will write these down in my prayer journal as a reminder that Jesus is always with me, no matter what.

January 4
ST. ELIZABETH ANN SETON,
RELIGIOUS (1774–1821)

Live simply, so that all may simply live.

—Traditionally attributed to St. Elizabeth Ann Seton

Today, I will do an examination of conscience according to this teaching and ask myself these questions: What two virtues are implicit in this quotation? To what extent has a consumerist mentality prevented me from living these virtues? What positive steps can I take, beginning today, to remedy this situation?

January 5
ST. JOHN NEUMANN, BISHOP (1811–1860)

*A man must always be ready, for death
comes when and where God wills it.*

—Reported last words of St. John Neumann

If today should be the day the Lord would call me home, would I be ready? What are my outstanding sins? Whose forgiveness do I need to ask? Whom do I need to forgive? What would be the last words my loved ones would remember me saying to them?

THE LIFE OF ST. ELIZABETH ANN SETON

B orn Elizabeth Ann Bayley in New York City, Mother Seton is a saint of firsts: first American-born saint, leader of the first Catholic girls' school (and the first free Catholic school of any kind) in the United States, and foundress of the first American order of religious sisters—the Sisters of Charity.

Elizabeth was born into a prominent Anglican family and was married in the Anglican Church. With her sister-in-law, Rebecca, she tended to the poor around New York, earning a reputation for her compassion and mercy. In 1803, she traveled to Italy with her ailing husband in the hope that the climate would aid his recovery.

William Seton died in Italy later that year, but in her grief Elizabeth discovered a new love: the Catholic Church. She scandalized her Protestant family and friends by being received into the Church in New York City on Ash Wednesday, 1805.

Finding New York no longer hospitable to her Catholic zeal, Elizabeth suffered through some trying years before finding a haven in Baltimore. It was there that she channeled her passion for service into girls' education. She also pursued her dream of religious life, fashioning a rudimentary habit in the style of nuns she had seen in Italy. Other women were drawn to her, and in 1809 the Sisters of Charity was born, based on the example of St. Vincent de Paul.

Mother Seton died in 1821 in Emmitsburg, Maryland, where her school still stands. In her refusal to let the social pressures of her station restrain her witness to the Catholic Faith—in word *and* deed—she is a wonderful example for us in a secularizing world.

January 6

SOLEMNITY OF THE EPIPHANY
OF OUR LORD

Look up, sweet Babe, look up and see
For love of Thee
Thus far from home
The east is come
To seek herself in Thy sweet eyes;
We, who strangely went astray,
Lost in a bright
Meridian night,
A darkness made of too much day,
Beckon'd from far
By Thy fair star,
Lo at last have found our way.

—Richard Crashaw: *The Glorious Epiphany*
of Our Lord (seventeenth century)

A brilliant star led the Magi to the manger of the Child Jesus. What (or who) have been the stars in my life that have led me to Jesus? I will say a prayer of thanksgiving for all these stars who have helped me grow in relationship with Our Lord.

January 7

With the help and blessing of God, we shall do all in our power that our new family may be a little cenacle where Jesus may reign over all affections, desires and actions.

—From a letter of St. Gianna Beretta Molla to her fiancé

To what extent would my home be described as a "little cenacle," or retreat house? What one action can I take today to make it more so?

January 8

*The sweet fragrance of Christ noticed among men [is]
not in a sudden burst of flame, but in the constant
red-hot embers of virtues such as justice, loyalty,
faithfulness, understanding, and cheerfulness.*

—St. Josemaría Escrivá, *Christ Is Passing By*

What is St. Josemaría communicating about an authentic witness to Christ in this quotation? Of the virtues listed above, which are "red-hot" in me? Which are growing cold, and in what specific way today can I heat them up?

January 9

*What are our real trials? By what name shall we call them?
One cuts herself out a cross of pride; another, one of causeless
discontent; another, one of restless impatience or peevish
fretfulness. Yet we know certainly that our God calls us
to a holy life, that he gives us every grace, every abundant
grace; and though we are weak of ourselves, this grace is
able to carry us through every obstacle and difficulty.*

—From a conference by St. Elizabeth Ann Seton

Have I cut out a cross for myself—one that I have fashioned rather than the Lord? Could this be why this cross is so heavy? Today, I will lay down before Our Lord this cross of my own fashioning, knowing and trusting that He is giving me the grace to carry the cross He has placed upon my shoulder.

January 10
FEAST OF THE BAPTISM OF OUR LORD

Like Saint Teresa, with five pennies and God,
I can accomplish many great things.

—Traditionally attributed to St. Frances Cabrini

Sometimes I feel as if I can accomplish nothing. But we all have "five pennies" that can accomplish so much when given to God. What are mine? What natural gifts and talents, personality characteristics and attributes, virtues and strengths can I put into the service of God? How can I implement at least one of them today?

January 11

*Believe that He loves you, that He wants to help
you in the struggles you have to undergo. Believe in
His love, His exceeding love, as St. Paul says.*

—From a letter of St. Elizabeth of the Trinity

We often fail to recognize God's love because we don't look for it in the midst of our struggles or in our everyday circumstances. Thus, our belief that God loves us often turns to doubt. How did God manifest His love for me in at least one way yesterday? With this thought in mind, I will seek to recognize His love for me in at least three ways today. In my evening prayer, I will thank Him, and I will close my eyes comforted by His warm embrace.

January 12

*We must become holy, not because we want to feel holy,
but because Christ must be able to live His life fully in us.*

—St. Teresa of Calcutta, reported by Malcolm
Muggeridge in *Something Beautiful for God*

How fully is Christ able to live His life in me? Do I give Him space to live and to grow, or do I stifle Him with my own will and desires?

January 13
ST. HILARY, BISHOP AND DOCTOR OF THE CHURCH (CA. 310–CA. 367)

I am well aware, almighty God and Father, that in my life I owe you a most particular duty. It is to make my every thought and word speak of you.

—From a homily of St. Hilary

Do I, like St. Hilary, consider it a duty to make my every thought and word speak of God? Why or why not? How can practicing the virtues accomplish this in a practical way?

January 14

A living love hurts. Jesus, to prove His love for us, died on the Cross. The mother, to give to her child, has to suffer. If you really love one another properly, there must be sacrifice.

—St. Teresa of Calcutta, reported by Malcolm Muggeridge in *Something Beautiful for God*

Where is God asking me to sacrifice in love right now? For whom? How can I live this out today, even in little ways?

THIS IS THE DAY
THE LORD HAS MADE

Many years ago I was preparing to lead a day of recollection for a group of people engaged in parish ministry. I rose early that morning to spend time before the Blessed Sacrament in the chapel of the retreat house where I was staying.

It was a lovely moment, filled with grace and consolation. This was especially comforting because it was the first time I had addressed a group like this and I was a bit apprehensive. In the confines of this holy place, I poured out my heart to the Lord.

Deep down in my soul, where St. Francis de Sales says we "hear the voice of God," I heard these words from Psalm 118:24: "This is the day the LORD has made, let us rejoice and be glad in it."

With lightning speed, I understood what the Holy Spirit was communicating! The day of recollection that I was going to embark upon had already been made by the Lord. He had meticulously planned this day from before the very foundations of the world had been laid in place! All I had to do was to be open to Him and to show up!

My friend, today is the day the Lord has made. He has ordained this day for you. Nothing that happens this day is outside of His will for you. Praise Him. Thank Him. Rejoice in Him. Be glad. Be open. And watch the marvels unfold.

January 15

My whole strength lies in prayer and sacrifice, these are my invincible arms; they can move hearts far better than words. I know it by experience.

—St. Thérèse of Lisieux, *Story of a Soul*

What makes prayer and sacrifice "invincible arms"? Whose heart have I been praying for? Am I willing to trust St. Thérèse's experience and enter into spiritual battle through prayer and sacrifice for this person?

January 16

---

*Let all bitterness and wrath and anger and clamor
and slander be put away from you, with all malice,
and be kind to one another, tenderhearted, forgiving
one another, as God in Christ forgave you.*

—Ephesians 4:31–32

The first sentence in this passage from Scripture lists many of the spiritual viruses that plague our soul. The second sentence provides the spiritual medicine to eradicate them. Which virus do I need to get rid of, and which spiritual remedy listed can I use?

January 17
ST. ANTHONY, ABBOT (CA. 250–356)

Indeed, he was so attentive when Scripture was read that nothing escaped him, and because he retained all he heard, his memory served him in place of books.

—From a life of St. Anthony by St. Athanasius

How attentive am I when I hear Sacred Scripture being read? Could I pass a pop quiz on the passage as soon as it is read? How about twenty-four hours later? How can I seek to be more attentive?

January 18

All holiness and perfection of soul lies in our love for Jesus Christ our God, who is our Redeemer and our supreme good. It is part of the love of God to acquire and to nurture all the virtues which make a man perfect.

—From a homily of St. Alphonsus Liguori

Which virtue do I most need to acquire? How do I know this? Am I willing to practice it to show my love of God?

January 19

*Let us not look too far or too high, but right in
front of ourselves, right next to ourselves.
The good to be done is perhaps there.*

—Servant of God Elisabeth Leseur,
The Secret Diary of Elisabeth Leseur

What "good to be done" today is right in front of me, right next to me? How can I accomplish this good today, even if just in little ways?

January 20
ST. SEBASTIAN, MARTYR (THIRD CENTURY)

---

*If there are many persecutions, there are many testings;
where there are many crowns of victory, there are
many trials of strength. It is then to your advantage if
there are many persecutors; among many persecutions
you may more easily find a path to victory.*

—From a homily of St. Ambrose on St. Sebastian

What "path to victory" have I found in past persecutions? How does this help me seek the path to victory in my current trial?

January 21
ST. AGNES, VIRGIN AND MARTYR (CA. 291–CA. 304)

I will be His who first chose me for Himself.

—St. Agnes at her martyrdom

God has chosen me for Himself just as He chose St. Agnes. Am I willing to choose Him first in all things? What one choice is He asking me to make today? What is my response?

January 22
ST. VINCENT, DEACON AND MARTYR (D. 304)

Against Christ's army the world arrays a twofold battle line. It offers temptation to lead us astray; it strikes terror into us to break our spirit. . . . At both of these approaches, Christ rushes to our aid, and the Christian is not conquered.

—From a homily of St. Augustine on St. Vincent

What is the twofold battle line on which I am currently engaged? Can I name one grace Christ is bringing to me so that I am not conquered?

January 23

Do not accept anything as the truth if it lacks love.
And do not accept anything as love which lacks truth!
One without the other becomes a destructive lie.

—St. John Paul II at the canonization of
St. Teresa Benedicta of the Cross (Edith Stein)

Have I seen in the lives of others the reality of this quote? To what extent do my own understandings of *love* and *truth* need to be redefined? Have I fallen victim to a *destructive lie* due to my false definitions? I ask the Holy Spirit to guide me to all that is true, all that is lovely, and all that is pure.

January 24
ST. FRANCIS DE SALES, BISHOP AND DOCTOR OF THE CHURCH (1567–1622)

Our business is to love what God would have done. He wills our vocation as it is. Let us love that and not trifle away our time hankering after other people's vocations.

—From a letter of St. Francis de Sales

How can "hankering after other people's vocations" lead me to be discontented with what God has chosen for me? How does it deprive me of grace? In what ways can it lead me into sin?

January 25
CONVERSION OF ST. PAUL, APOSTLE

For the sake of Christ, then, I am content with weaknesses, insults, hardships, persecutions, and calamities; for when I am weak, then I am strong.

—2 Corinthians 12:10

Dear St. Paul, I wish I could say that I am content with weakness, mistreatment, distress, persecution, and difficulties, but that is not the case. All too often I complain at the least struggle or trial. Pray for me that I obtain the grace I need to endure all things for the sake of Christ. Help me to see that when I am most powerless, Christ can fortify me if I surrender my suffering to Him. May the strength of Christ fill me, and may I embrace the Cross with valor and conviction.

January 26
STS. TIMOTHY AND TITUS,
BISHOPS (FIRST CENTURY)

*As for you, always be steady, endure suffering, do
the work of an evangelist, fulfill your ministry.*

—2 Timothy 4:5

How can I fulfill my ministry of evangelization today in at least one way?

January 27
ST. ANGELA MERICI, VIRGIN (1470–1540)

Mothers and sisters most dear to me in Christ: in the first place strive with all your power and zeal to be open. With the help of God, try to receive such good counsel that, led solely by the love of God and an eagerness to save souls, you may fulfill your charge. Only if the responsibilities committed to you are rooted in this twofold charity will they bear beneficial and saving fruit.

—St. Angela Merici, *Spiritual Testament*

To what extent are the responsibilities committed to me rooted in the twofold charity St. Angela Merici recommends? How can I help these roots to grow?

January 28

ST. THOMAS AQUINAS, PRIEST
AND DOCTOR (1225–1274)

Whoever wishes to live perfectly should do nothing but disdain what Christ disdained on the Cross and desire what he desired, for the Cross exemplifies every virtue.

—From a conference by St. Thomas Aquinas

What virtues do I see exemplified by Jesus on the Cross? What did Jesus disdain on the Cross? What did He desire? What virtues do I see exemplified by Jesus on the Cross? In what ways can I follow them?

THE LIFE OF ST. ANGELA MERICI

St. Angela Merici, born in 1474 in northern Italy, had a tumultuous early life. She was orphaned in her teens and went with her sisters to live with her uncle. While there, one of her sisters died suddenly before she could receive the Last Rites. Angela prayed fervently for her sister's soul, and it is said that she received a vision of her sister in Heaven.

Shortly thereafter her uncle died as well, and Angela returned to her hometown. She had previously joined the Third Order of St. Francis, and now she consecrated herself to God.

She was considered quite beautiful, and so in order to avoid unwanted attention from the young men of her town, she dyed her hair with soot.

St. Angela's greatest legacy is the Ursuline Order. While the Ursulines are now cloistered nuns, Angela founded the group as the Company of St. Ursula, named for the patron of medieval education.

The Company was unique for the time in that the women lived in their homes among their families and wore no special attire. Angela's intention was to build up women in the Faith so that they could form strong Catholic families and pass down the Faith to their children. Soon, the charism of the order expanded to girls' education and service to the poor.

The Company of St. Ursula grew rapidly until St. Angela's death in 1540. She is a beautiful example for women (and men!) of creativity, innovation, and obedience in the service of the Church.

January 29

The way to destroy bad habits is by watchfulness and by doing often those things that are opposites to one's besetting sins.

—From a homily of St. John Vianney

What one bad habit is the Holy Spirit giving me the grace to overcome? What virtue is the opposite of it? In what three ways can I begin to exercise that virtue?

January 30

---

*Finally, brethren, whatever is true, whatever is honorable,
whatever is just, whatever is pure, whatever is lovely,
whatever is gracious, if there is any excellence, if there
is anything worthy of praise, think about these things.
What you have learned and received and heard and seen
in me, do; and the God of peace will be with you.*

—Philippians 4:8–9

To what extent do I take custody of my imagination and my thoughts? What patterns of thinking do I need to replace with more noble thoughts?

THE LIFE OF ST. JOHN BOSCO

St. John Bosco was born in 1815 into a poor family in the Italian countryside. His father died at an early age, and John's childhood work as a shepherd impeded his deep desire to learn about the Catholic Faith. He left home at the age of twelve after repeated confrontations with his older brother, and in 1835 he entered the seminary.

From an early age John had a passion for helping wayward boys. Industrialization had devastated the countryside and led to incredible misery in the cities—including Turin, where he settled. Many boys found themselves in prisons for petty crimes, and many more wandered the streets.

Fr. Bosco established an oratory, or house of prayer, to give the boys of Turin shelter, peace, and education. He started in 1842 with about twenty boys; in just a few years, he had hundreds under his care. Naturally, neighbors and local leaders complained about everything from the racket of the boys' playing to the possibility that Fr. Bosco was developing a revolutionary army. But he persevered, moving his oratory several times.

St. John Bosco may be best remembered today for his methods for educating and disciplining troublesome boys. He focused always on love and kindness and felt in particular that games and music were essential to teaching and civilizing youngsters.

Owing to his great devotion to St. Francis de Sales, Fr. Bosco founded an organization known as the Salesians to spread his work. By the time of his death in 1888, more than a hundred thousand boys were living and growing in faith in Salesian houses around the world.

January 31
ST. JOHN BOSCO, PRIEST (1815–1888)

There must be no hostility in our minds, no contempt in our eyes, no insult on our lips. We must use mercy for the present and have hope for the future, as is fitting for true fathers who are eager for real correction and improvement.

—From a letter of St. John Bosco on disciplining boys

How can I apply this advice in my dealings with children — mine or those entrusted to me? How does this advice apply to my actions with all people?

Chapter Two

Meditations

FOR

FEBRUARY

February 1

When the Lord knows that good health is necessary
for our welfare, He sends it to us; and when
we need sickness, He sends that too.

— Traditionally attributed to St. Teresa of Ávila

Can I think of a time in my own life (or in another's life) when sickness was a blessing? What spiritual benefits did it bring? "We know that in everything God works for good with those who love him, who are called according to his purpose" (Romans 8:28).

February 2

PRESENTATION OF THE LORD

Behold, this child is set for the fall and rising of many in Israel, and for a sign that is spoken against (and a sword will pierce through your own soul also), that thoughts out of many hearts may be revealed.

—Luke 2:34–35

How have some of my "secret thoughts" found their way into the Immaculate Heart of Mary, and how has she responded? Consider those sufferings, trials, prayers of petition, and loved ones you have entrusted to her.

February 3
ST. BLASE (D. 316)

*O God, deliver us through the intercession of Thy holy
bishop and martyr Blase, from all evil of soul and body,
especially from all ills of the throat; and grant us the
grace to make a good confession in the confident hope of
obtaining Thy pardon, and ever to praise with worthy lips
Thy most holy name. Through Christ our Lord. Amen.*

—From the Novena Prayer to St. Blase

What "evil of soul and body" do I specifically wish to
entrust to the intercession of St. Blase today?

THE LIFE OF ST. BLASE

While many of the details of the life of St. Blase are lost to history, we know that in the early fourth century he was a bishop in what is today central Turkey, where he was martyred. While he was little known in his own day, Blase became one of the most popular saints in medieval Europe, with churches and shrines dedicated to him across the continent. Many of the stories passed down about St. Blase are based on legendary stories from this era.

The great medieval devotion to Blase seems to have been based on the tradition that, before becoming a bishop, he was a physician to whom miraculous healings were attributed — most notably the curing of a boy with a fishbone in his throat. In churches around the world to this day, St. Blase's feast is celebrated by the blessing of throats, usually with two candles tied together to form a cross and placed on the throat. Blase remains a popular intercessor for all manner of illnesses.

It is said that when the Roman persecutors came for Blase, he was found praying in a cave surrounded by animals who came for his blessing and to help him. His legend indicates that he endured many forms of torture, including "combing," in which the body is raked and flayed with the large iron combs used to prepare wool. (For this reason he is the patron saint of wool combers.) Refusing to renounce his faith, St. Blase was beheaded in the year 316.

February 4

The act and spirit of giving are the best counter to the evil forces in the world today, and giving liberates the individual not only spiritually but materially.

—Dorothy Day, *Loaves and Fishes*

Why is generosity both a liberator of the individual and an effective "counter" to the spirit of the world? How can I practice this virtue with greater consistency and love?

February 5

ST. AGATHA, VIRGIN AND MARTYR (THIRD CENTURY)

She wore the glow of a pure conscience and the crimson of the Lamb's blood for her cosmetics.... Her robe is the mark of her faithful witness to Christ.

—From a homily of St. Methodius on St. Agatha

To what extent is my conscience pure? To what extent do I gratefully bear the blood of the Lamb in and through my struggles and trials? Would someone regard me as a faithful witness to Christ? Why or why not?

February 6

Someone has said we do not save others by changing and converting and developing them; we redeem them by the love that accepts them and serves them as they are.

—From the journal of Sister Miriam of the
Holy Spirit, O.C.D. (Jessica Powers)

Who is that one person in my life whom I have been trying to change and convert by "developing them"? In what ways have I tried to do this? What better way does the quote suggest? How can I begin to change my approach?

February 7

Suffering borne in the will quietly and patiently is a continual, very powerful prayer before God.

—From a letter of St. Jane Frances de Chantal
to her brother, the Archbishop of Bourges

The question should not be: "Will I suffer?" I am assured of that by living in a fallen world. Rather, the question should be: "What will I do when I suffer?" What does St. Jane Frances de Chantal recommend that I do? What do I think it means to bear suffering "in the will"?

February 8
ST. JOSEPHINE BAKHITA, VIRGIN (1869–1947)

*If I were to meet the slave-traders who kidnapped
me and even those who tortured me, I would kneel
and kiss their hands, for if that did not happen, I
would not be a Christian and religious today.*

—St. Josephine Bakhita, reported by Maria
Dagnino in *Bakhita Tells Her Story*

Have I been persecuted, betrayed, or treated unjustly? What
great good has God worked out of my tragedy? I pray
for the eyes to see.

February 9

The perfection of a Christian consists in knowing how to mortify himself for the love of Christ. . . . Where there is no great mortification there is no great sanctity.

—From the maxims of St. Philip Neri

How is God asking me to mortify myself that I might be filled more with the things of God than the things of the world? How does this show my love of Christ and lead to greater sanctity?

THE LIFE OF ST. JOSEPHINE BAKHITA

St. Josephine Bakhita was born into a respected family in the late 1860s in the Darfur region of western Sudan. Before her tenth birthday, however, she was kidnapped by Arab slave traders and marched more than six hundred miles to the markets in central Sudan. She lost her birth name and couldn't remember it after her abduction, so she was given the name *Bakhita*—Arabic for "lucky."

Compelled to convert to Islam, Bakhita served several masters, including an Arab merchant and a Turkish general whose wife and mother-in-law cruelly tormented her. As an Islamic revolution fomented in Sudan, the Turkish general left the country and sold Bakhita to an Italian statesman. The Italian,

Callisto Legnani, treated her well and took her with him to Genoa when he too fled Sudan in 1885.

In Italy, Bakhita was given to friends of Legnani, the Michielis, who lived near Venice. When her new mistress traveled back to Africa to join her husband there, Bakhita stayed behind in the care of the Canossian Sisters in Venice. There, Bakhita fell in love with the Lord. When Michieli returned to Italy she refused to leave the convent, and in late 1889 an Italian court ruled that Bakhita could not be held as a slave in Italy.

In his encyclical *Spe Salvi* (*Saved in Hope*), Pope Benedict XVI writes of St. Josephine Bakhita: "Through the knowledge of this hope she was 'redeemed,' no longer a slave, but a free child of God." In early 1890 she was baptized and confirmed with the name Josephine. Six years later she took her vows with the Canossians, with whom she lived in faith and humility for fifty years, traveling around Italy promoting the cause of missionary work.

February 10

The way of faith gives us more than the way of philosophical thought: it gives us God, near to us as person, who loves us and deals with us mercifully, giving us that security which human knowledge cannot give. But the way of faith is dark.

—St. Teresa Benedicta of the Cross (Edith Stein), *Finite and Eternal Being*

What do I think St. Teresa Benedicta of the Cross means by "the way of faith is dark"?

February 11

OUR LADY OF LOURDES

I am the Immaculate Conception.

—The Blessed Virgin to St. Bernadette Soubirous

Do I understand the meaning of the dogma of the Immaculate Conception—that Mary was conceived without the blemish of original sin? I will ask the Blessed Mother today to enhance my appreciation of this great truth.

February 12

If you would attain the purity you ask of me, there are three principal things you must do. You must be united with me in loving affection, bearing in your memory the blessings you have received from me. With the eye of your understanding you must see my affectionate charity, how unspeakably much I love you. And when the human will is concerned you must consider my will rather than people's evil intentions, for I am their judge — not you, but I.

—Our Lord to St. Catherine of Siena, *The Dialogue*

What are the three things Our Lord told St. Catherine of Siena she must do to attain purity? How was she to acquire each? Of the three, which one do I most need to attain now? How can I do so?

February 13

What do you think His will is? The Lord asks of us only two things: love of His Majesty and love of our neighbor. These are what we must work for. By keeping them with perfection, we do His will and so will be united with Him.

—St. Teresa of Ávila, *The Interior Castle*

In what way is this quote meant especially for me today? How can I come to appreciate the Majesty of the Lord more?

February 14

Love is the key to the mystery. Love by its very nature is not selfish, but generous. It seeks not its own, but the good of others. The measure of love is not the pleasure it gives—that is the way the world judges it—but the joy and peace it can purchase for others.

—Ven. Fulton J. Sheen, *The Rainbow of Sorrow*

Love is not an emotion as much as it is a decision of the will. How can I show love today according to this quote?

February 15

---

*It is amusing to see souls who, while they are at prayer,
fancy they are willing to be despised and publicly insulted
for the love of God, yet afterward do all they can to
hide their small defects; if anyone unjustly accuses
them of a fault, God deliver us from their outcries!*

—St. Teresa of Ávila, *The Interior Castle*

This is a hard truth from St. Teresa. If I'm being honest with myself, to what extent does this describe me?

February 16

One of the favorite images I like to use for describing the Christian life is of a person standing with arms outstretched. One hand, in faith and prayer, touches God; the other hand is extended in service to the neighbor. Thus a person is cruciform, touching God and touching neighbor.

—Catherine de Hueck Doherty, *Poustinia*

How does this quotation speak of spiritual motherhood? How can I be cruciform today?

February 17

THE SEVEN FOUNDERS OF THE ORDER OF SERVITES (THIRTEENTH CENTURY)

In the beginning our Lady was the chief architect of this new order which was founded on the humility of its members, built up by their mutual love, and preserved by their poverty.

Legenda de Origine of the Order of
Servants of the Blessed Virgin Mary

Is the Blessed Mother the "architect" of my hopes and dreams, my plans and my way of life? How can I entrust everything to her?

February 18

God said: *"Why do you never stop asking to taste of My delights, yet you refuse the tribulations?"*

—Traditionally attributed to St. Margaret of Cortona

This is a good question to ask myself. What is my response?

February 19

For I will only your well-being, and whatever I give, I give it so that you may reach the goal for which I created you.

—Our Lord to St. Catherine of Siena, *The Dialogue*

I t is easy to see God's hand in the good things of our lives, but it is often a struggle to see it in the difficult. How do these words of Our Lord to St. Catherine of Siena give me deeper insight? In what way does this help me to reexamine past events or a current situation?

February 20

He did not say: You will not be troubled; you will not be tempted; you will not be distressed. But He said: You will not be overcome.

—St. Juliana of Norwich, *Showings*

Dear Lord, so often I feel all but swallowed up by the events of everyday life—not to mention those difficult moments of struggle, confusion, and doubt. It is Your grace and Your grace alone that gets me through these moments. Help me to remember that in the midst of every circumstance, You are there. In the midst of every reversal, You are there. In my deepest pain, in my worst distress, in my greatest temptation, You are there. Help me to hold on to this truth, and in You I will overcome. Amen.

February 21

ST. PETER DAMIEN, BISHOP AND DOCTOR (1007–1072)

In serenity, look forward to the joy that follows sadness.
Hope leads you to that joy and love enkindles your zeal.

—From a letter of St. Peter Damien

The letter to the Hebrews tells us that "faith is the assurance of things hoped for, the conviction of things not seen" (11:1). How does this help me live out the advice of St. Peter Damien?

GOD WANTS THE WORST FROM US

Not long ago, a woman shared with me that she had received a beautiful gift from the Lord on her birthday. During her prayer time she seemed to "hear" the voice of God deep down in the inner recesses of her heart:

"Let me love you, my daughter. Let me love you in those areas of pain, in those areas of shame, in those areas that seem to be the refuse of your life. Let me love you there."

I could relate to her words.

I once had heard something similar in my own time of evening prayer. I had been complaining to the Lord that I had nothing to offer Him that night. It seemed that it had been a day more laden with frailties and weaknesses than gifts and strengths. As I lamented, I seemed to hear Our Lord say, "What I want from you is your frailty and weakness. Don't you see? That is all you have to offer me. Anything that is good in you is me already."

What an amazing word! What a gift to see!

God wants all of us. He desires to make us His dwelling place, His tabernacle, His holy temple. If we surrender to Him all of those areas of pain, sin, weakness, and imperfection—all of our debris and refuse—He can enter us more fully, transform us more completely, and conform us to His image more closely.

What are your areas of refuse? Where have you stuffed your debris? Surrender it all to God.

February 22

THE CHAIR OF ST. PETER

And I tell you, you are Peter, and on this rock
I will build my church, and the powers of
death shall not prevail against it.

—Matthew 16:18

How have I seen the truth of this statement in light of the history of the Church? How does this speak to the fact that the Catholic Church is the Church Jesus founded?

February 23

ST. POLYCARP, BISHOP AND MARTYR (D. 155)

Leave me as I am. The one who gives me strength to endure the fire will also give me strength to stay quite still on the pyre, even without the precaution of your nails.

—St. Polycarp at his martyrdom

How is God giving me the strength of endurance today?

February 24

Very well, I will be a saint. I will provide a patron for those who bear my name.

—Bl. Dina Belanger, from her autobiography

At age eight, Dina Belanger said this in response to a teacher who told her the Church had no St. Dina. Am I willing to "provide a patron" for those who bear my name? What positive step can I take today to make that happen?

February 25

It is good when a soul loves solitude; it's a sign that it takes delight in God and enjoys speaking with Him.

—From a letter of St. Jane Frances de Chantal
to her brother, Archbishop of Bourges

How do I respond to solitude? Do I embrace it or flee from it? What does this tell me about my interior life and my relationship with God?

February 26

Speak little to creatures but speak much to God. He will make you truly wise.

—From a letter of St. Mary Mazzarello

Of the words I speak each day, what percentage do I speak to God and what percentage do I speak to creatures? Am I happy with these totals, especially in light of the gift of wisdom?

February 27

The love of talk distracts all the powers of our soul from God and fills them with earthly objects and impressions like a vessel of water which cannot be clear and settled while you are continually stirring the earthly particles from the bottom.

—St. Elizabeth Ann Seton to her Sisters of Charity

The powers of the soul are will, reason, and emotion. How can the "love of talk" draw these away from God? To what extent have I seen this to be true in myself? What practical strategies can I use to purge myself of this tendency?

February 28

It is not our perfection which is to dazzle God, Who is surrounded by myriads of angels. No, it is our misery, our wretchedness avowed which draws down His mercy.

—Bl. Columba Marmion, "Humility Is Walking in the Truth"

Our misery and wretchedness draws down God's mercy. What sadness or situation, circumstance or travail do I want to surrender to Him today so as to experience God's mercy in the midst of it?

Chapter Three

Meditations

FOR

MARCH

March 1

*By being close to Christ in the sacraments and in prayer,
we can fulfill our great feminine vocation: to live out
our love for others day by day in faithfulness.*

—Ronda Chervin, *Feminine, Free, and Faithful*

To what extent has a life of prayer and reception of the sacraments impacted my feminine vocation? In what one way can I seek to improve my faithfulness?

March 2

---

*In all talking and conversation let something
always be said of spiritual things, and so shall all
idle words and evil speaking be avoided.*

—From the maxims of St. Teresa of Ávila

According to this statement of St. Teresa of Ávila, how do I evaluate my conversations with others? Uplifting or downgrading?

March 3

ST. KATHARINE DREXEL (1858–1955)

O Mary, make me endeavor, by all the means in my power, to extend the kingdom of your Divine Son and offer incessantly my prayers for the conversion of those who are yet in darkness or estranged from His fold.

—From the writings of St. Katharine Drexel

How can I, with Mother Mary's help, "extend the kingdom" of Jesus in my daily life?

THE LIFE OF ST. KATHARINE DREXEL

St. Katharine Drexel, the only saint to have been an American citizen from birth, was born in 1858 into one of the most prominent families in Philadelphia. Her paternal grandfather had founded Drexel University, and her father was a nationally recognized banker.

From a young age, Katharine, her sister Elizabeth, and her half-sister Emma shared a passion for service that permeated the Drexel family. The clan would regularly hand out food and financial assistance from their Philadelphia mansion—and they would seek out those who were too ashamed to approach them.

As a young woman, Katharine developed a particular interest in the struggles of black Americans in the South and of

Native Americans across the West. Katharine and her sisters used her family's fortune to fund Franciscan missions in South Dakota and elsewhere; meanwhile, she began to consider entering religious life.

In 1887, the three sisters were granted a private audience by Pope Leo XIII in Rome. The pope encouraged Katharine to take up missionary work herself. She entered the Sisters of Mercy in Pittsburgh in 1889 and within a few years had founded and funded, using her family's inheritance, the Sisters of the Blessed Sacrament.

This distinctively American order of women religious was dedicated to the service of neglected Black and Native American populations around the country—with a special focus on education. By the time of her death in 1955, St. Katharine Drexel had founded fifty missions in sixteen states. Her Sisters of the Blessed Sacrament continue to serve and to educate the poorest of the poor across the United States.

March 4

ST. CASIMIR (1461–1484)

Daily, daily sing to Mary,
Sing, my soul, her praises due:
All her feasts, her actions honor
With the heart's devotion true.

Lost in wond'ring contemplation,
Be her majesty confessed:
Call her Mother, call her Virgin,
Happy Mother, Virgin blest.

She is mighty in her pleading,
Tender in her loving care;
Ever watchful, understanding,
All our sorrows she will share.

Advocate and loving mother,
Mediatrix of all grace:

Heaven's blessings she dispenses
On our sinful human race.

All our graces flow through Mary;
All then join her praise to sing:
Fairest work of all creation,
Mother of creation's King.

Sing in songs of peace unending,
Call upon her lovingly:
Seat of wisdom, Gate of heaven,
Morning star upon the sea.

—A copy of this hymn by Bernard of Cluny was
found beneath the right temple of St. Casimir's
incorrupt body when his grave was opened.

This song, treasured by St. Casimir, provides a catechesis
on the Blessed Mother as well as listing some of her most
well-known titles. What does this song teach us about Mary
and about various titles of Our Lady?

March 5

Women are called to bring to the family, to society, and to the Church characteristics which are their own and which they alone can give: their gentle warmth and untiring generosity, their love for detail, their quick-wittedness and intuition, their simple and deep piety, their constancy.

—St. Josemaría Escrivá, *Conversations*

In what specific ways do I demonstrate the feminine qualities listed by St. Josemaría Escrivá? In what new ways can I live them out?

March 6

Fear not. . . . I have called you by name, you are mine.

Isaiah 43:1

How are these words meant for me today?

March 7

To a great extent the level of any civilization is the level of its womanhood. When a man loves a woman, he has to become worthy of her. The higher her virtue, the more her character, the more devoted she is to truth, justice, goodness, the more a man has to aspire to be worthy of her. The history of civilization could actually be written in terms of the level of its women.

—Ven. Fulton J. Sheen, from his *Life Is Worth Living* television program

To what extent am I raising the level of our culture and civilization?

March 8

ST. JOHN OF GOD (1495–1550)

Every person must embrace the state for which God intends him. And parents should therefore not be so anxious and exercised over it but should rather pray to God to grant the state of grace to each of their sons and daughters.

—From a letter of St. John of God

Am I embracing the state for which God has intended me, or am I railing against it? What about with regard to my husband, children, and all of those entrusted to me? Do I entrust them to God, or do I try to do it all myself?

March 9

ST. FRANCES OF ROME (1384–1440)

She did not cease to be mindful of the things of God during her marriage, so that she pleased God in her husband and her husband in God.

—From the prayer book of the community of women founded by St. Frances of Rome

St. Frances of Rome did not want to marry but desired to enter religious life instead. She recognized, however, that marriage was God's will for her. She did marry, and, following the death of her husband, she founded a religious community. How is God speaking to me through the witness of the life of St. Frances of Rome?

March 10

Which stands up better in a crisis — man or woman? . . .
The best way to arrive at a conclusion is to go to the
greatest crisis the world ever faced, namely the Crucifixion
of our Divine Lord. When we come to this great
drama of Calvary there is one fact that stands out
very clearly: Men failed. . . . On the other hand, there
is not a single instance of a woman failing him.

—Ven. Fulton J. Sheen, *The World's First Love*

Am I willing to stand at the foot of the Cross with Mary and the other holy women? What cross is mine today?

THE LIFE OF ST. FRANCES OF ROME

Born in Rome in 1384, St. Frances demonstrated a love of the Lord from a young age. When her prominent parents overruled her desire to become a nun, at the age of twelve she acquiesced to the marriage they arranged.

Frances lived through difficult times for Rome and for the Church as a succession of antipopes claimed the chair of St. Peter. Frances's husband, Lorenzo Ponziani, was a commander of papal soldiers always loyal to the true pope, but the constant fighting devastated Rome and kept Lorenzo away from home.

Alone in a dangerous city, Frances threw herself into works of charity. Much to the chagrin of her father-in-law, she often distributed the family's money and goods to the poor. It is said that he retracted his complaint when the family's storehouses were miraculously replenished through Frances's prayers.

Frances's detachment from worldly concerns attracted many wealthy Roman women to her works, and so she founded an association of women attached to a local Benedictine monastery. With neither vows nor a rule of life, the women were free to live in the world while committing themselves to prayer and service. For those who desired a community life, in 1433 Frances founded a monastery that functions to this day.

St. Frances of Rome's commitment to bodily mortification was legendary. She ate little and wore horse-hair garments. This commitment to detachment was rewarded by the Lord with fabulous visions, including regular conversations with her guardian angel. Through it all she lived with her doting husband until his death in 1436, when she moved into her monastery. She died there in 1440.

March 11

*Never utter in your neighbor's absence what
you would not say in their presence.*

—Traditionally attributed to St. Mary Magdalene de Pazzi

How well do I heed this sage advice?

March 12

The isolation of my soul, the constant and painful
injuries caused by those who are hostile or indifferent,
especially when they are near and dear to me, the sadness
of feeling unequal to the great task to be accomplished,
the sufferings of my heart, the difficulties of my life,
the misery of my physical weakness—this is the rugged
soil, my God, in which Thou wilt cause joy to grow.

—Servant of God Elisabeth Leseur,
The Secret Diary of Elisabeth Leseur

What is the "soil" out of which God desires to grow joy in my life?

March 13

*The soul about to receive Holy Communion should
be pure, that it may be purified; alive, that it may be
quickened; just, that it may be justified; ready, that it may
be incorporated with God uncreated who was made Man,
and that it may be one with Him unto all eternity.*

—St. Angela of Foligno, *Book of Divine Consolation*

What is the state of my soul today? Am I ready to receive
Holy Communion?

March 14

Let us therefore give ourselves to God with a great desire to begin to live thus, and beg Him to destroy in us the life of the world of sin, and to establish His life within us.

—Traditionally attributed to St. John Eudes

What one area of my life do I have need to establish the life of God? What one step can I take today to begin?

March 15

It is human to fall, but angelic to rise again.

—St. Mary Euphrasia Pelletier, *Conferences and Instructions*

Where does this bring hope to me today?

March 16

You must pray the prayer of action, which is the fragrant flower of the soul. A good man is a prayer.

—St. Catherine of Siena, reported in *St. Catherine of Siena* by Alice Curtayne

---

Why is the prayer of action "the fragrant flower of the soul"? Am I a prayer?

March 17

ST. PATRICK, BISHOP (385–461)

Christ shield me this day: Christ with me, Christ before me, Christ behind me, Christ in me, Christ beneath me, Christ above me, Christ on my right, Christ on my left, Christ when I lie down, Christ when I arise, Christ in the heart of every person who thinks of me, Christ in the eye that sees me, Christ in the ear that hears me.

—Breastplate of St. Patrick

What "armor" do I wear daily? How convinced am I that I need to wear the armor of God? Consider this in light of these verses: "Put on the whole armor of God, that you may be able to stand against the wiles of the devil. For we are not contending against flesh and blood, but against the principalities, against the powers, against the world rulers of this present darkness, against the spiritual hosts of wickedness in the heavenly places. Therefore take the whole armor of God, that you may be able to withstand in the evil day, and having done all, to stand" (Ephesians 6:11–13).

March 18

ST. CYRIL OF JERUSALEM (315–386)

Confess what you have done in word or deed, by night or day. Confess in an acceptable time, and in the day of salvation receive the heavenly treasure.

—St. Cyril of Jerusalem, *Catechetical Lectures*

How does this quote speak to me specifically today? How recently have I gone to confession? Should I go more frequently?

March 19

SOLEMNITY OF SAINT JOSEPH, HUSBAND OF THE BLESSED VIRGIN MARY

Behold, an angel of the Lord appeared to Joseph in a dream and said, "Rise, take the child and his mother, and flee to Egypt, and remain there till I tell you." . . . And he rose and took the child and his mother by night, and departed to Egypt.

Matthew 2:13, 14

St. Joseph responded to the word of God immediately. How quickly do I respond to God's word and the promptings of the Holy Spirit? St. Joseph's obedience to God saved his family from calamity. Can I remember a time when my obedience to God saved me from some disaster or unfortunate situation? To what extent will this help me to obey God promptly today and in the future?

LENT: DEATH AND NEW LIFE

During Lent, Holy Mother Church directs us to ponder the reality of our mortality and, in light of that, to make a serious appraisal of how we are living.

In *Divine Intimacy*, Father Gabriel of St. Mary Magdalene, writes:

> Although death is the last, it is not the only coming of the Lord in the life of a Christian; it is preceded by many other comings whose special purpose is to prepare us for this last. Death will then be for us in the fullest sense a coming of grace.

What food for meditation these two sentences provide! They provoke us to consider the ways in which we have been "visited" by the Lord already. These visitations can be joyful or sorrowful; they might emerge from deep prayer or from times of spiritual dryness. But all of them prepare us for that final coming of the Lord that will take us into eternal life.

Later in the meditation, Father Gabriel tells us that an abiding love of God and conformity to His will in all things should be "the supreme norm of all our actions."

Is love of God and conformity to His will the primary motivator of all that I do? If not, what can be done about it?

We must beg God for a deeper love of Him—a movement of the Holy Spirit that illuminates our selfishness and pride and begins a process of restoration and renewal within us. This is the kind of visitation from the Lord we most need to experience. May it be one that marks a new beginning in Him—one that leads us to everlasting life.

Triduum

HOLY THURSDAY

Prone in Gethsemane upon His face, —
His eyelids closed, — lay Christ of all our world, —
The winds with endless sorrows seemed enswirled;
A little fountain murmured of its pain
Reflecting the pale sickle of the moon; —
Then was the hour when the Angel brought
From God's high throne the Cup of bitter horn,
While on His hands tears trembling fell like rain.
Before the Christ a cross arose on high;
He saw His own young body hanging there
Mangled, distorted; knotted ropes half-tear
The sinews from their sockets; saw He nigh
The jagged nails' hot rage, the direful Crown
Upon His head, and every dripping thorn
Red-laden, as in fury of its scorn
The thunder battered all kind voices down.

He heard the pattering drops, as from the cross
A piteous sobbing whispered and grew still.
Then Jesus sighed, and every pore did spill
A bloody sweat.

—Excerpt from "Gethsemane," Annette
Von Droste-Hulshoff (1797–1848)

Take this poem into your prayer-time meditation as you consider the great gift of our redemption. Then ask this question of yourself: "How is Jesus speaking to me through this poem?"

Triduum

GOOD FRIDAY

Jesus: O Mother dear, didst thou but hear
       My plaint of desolation,
       Thy tender heart would burst apart
       With grief of separation!

       I am not stone, yet all alone
       I hush My soul's outcrying, —
       Alone to tread the wine-press red,
       To bear the pain of dying.

       My lips are dumb, the night has come;
       Ah! Solace I might borrow
       Had I but thee to bide with Me
       In this wild waste of sorrow.

Mary: "Gentle moon and start of midnight,
       Day's fierce orb, and brooklets fair,

Golden apples born of sunshine,
Precious pearls and jewels rare, —
All things glorious, all things shining,"
Thus the sorrowing Mother spake;
"E'en ye bright, transfigured faces,
Mourn with me for Jesus' sake.

"Sparkle, gleam, and glow no longer:
Only moan and mourn for Him.
Shine not, shine not, weep forever,
Till your thousand eyes are dim;
For the mighty One has fallen,
And my Beautiful is slain;
In the dense wood pierced, my Shepherd, —
Weep ye, weep ye for my pain!
O most oppressed of all oppressed,
Heart of my heart, my all, my Son!
Grief's keenest sword doth pierce my breast:
I die with Thee, my only one!
Alas! The pain is all too great,
Since, living, still I share Thy fate.

"Yes, mine Thou wert to bear and rear
Through life and light, and pain and loss;
And now, ten thousand times more dear,
I yield Thee to the cruel cross!"

— "Dialogue at the Cross," Frederick Spee, S.J. (1591–1635),
translated from the German by Mary E. Mannix.)

Today I stand at the foot of the Cross with Mary my mother. What pain, sorrow, suffering, trial, and contradiction do I yield to the "cruel cross"? How does Mary give me guidance in this surrender?

Triduum

HOLY SATURDAY

I am not moved to love Thee, O my Lord,
By any longing for Thy Promised Land;
Nor by the fear of hell am I unmanned
To cease from my transgressing deed or word.
'Tis Thou Thyself dost move me, — Thy blood poured
Upon the cross from nailed foot and hand;
And all the wounds that did Thy body brand;
And all Thy shame and bitter death's award.

Yea, to Thy heart am I so deeply stirred
That I would love Thee were no heaven on high, —
That I would fear, were hell a tale absurd!
Such my desire, all questioning grows vain;
Though hope deny me hope I still should sigh,
And as my love is now, it should remain.

—"To Christ Crucified," anonymous (sixteenth or seventeenth century), translated from the Spanish by Thomas Walsh

On this Holy Saturday I enter into the tomb with Jesus. What one area of my life is most in need of resurrection? How is Jesus showing me that He wants to bring this part of me "back to life"?

Easter Sunday

Most glorious Lord of life that on this day
Didst make Thy triumph over death and sin,
And having harrowed hell didst bring away
Captivity thence captive us to win;
This joyous day, dear Lord, with joy begin
And grant that we, for whom Thou didst die
Being with Thy dear blood clean washed from sin,
May live forever in felicity.

And that Thy love we weighing worthily,
May likewise love Thee for the same again;
And for Thy sake that all like dear didst buy,
With love may one another entertain.
So let us love, dear love, like as we ought,
Love is the lesson which the Lord us taught.

— "Easter," Edmund Spenser (1553–1598)

JESUS LIVES! How am I experiencing His life in me on this glorious day?

March 20

O tender Father,
You gave me more, much more,
than I ever thought to ask for.
Thank you, and again thank you,
O Father,
for having granted my requests,
and for having granted those things
that I never realized
I needed or sought.

—A prayer of St. Catherine of Siena

Make a list of the petitions God has answered for you. Now make a list of the many blessings God has bestowed upon you for which you did not make an appeal. Praise and thank Him.

March 21

For the Christian there is no such thing as a "stranger".
Whoever is near us and needing us most is our "neighbor";
it does not matter whether he is related to us or not,
whether we like him or not, whether he is morally worthy
of our help or not. The love of Christ knows no limits.

—St. Teresa Benedicta of the Cross (Edith
Stein), "The Mystery of Christmas"

Today I will make a conscious effort to see what "neighbors" God brings into my life and in what ways they might need me.

March 22

*Manifest yourself. You have not time to occupy your
thoughts with that complacency or consideration
of what others will think. Your business is simply,
"What will my Father in Heaven think?"*

—From a letter of St. Katharine Drexel

In what one situation, circumstance, or personal relationship
do these words apply to me at this time? How can I now
respond to it?

March 23

Two criminals were crucified with Christ. One was saved; do not despair. One was not; do not presume.

—Traditionally attributed to St. Augustine

In what ways do I see myself in both criminals?

March 24

---

*From the depth of my nothingness, I prostrate myself
before Thee, O Most Sacred, Divine and Adorable
Heart of Jesus, to pay Thee all the homage of love,
praise and adoration in my power. Amen.*

—From a prayer to the Sacred Heart by
St. Margaret Mary Alacoque

What does the Sacred Heart of Jesus mean to me? How can I demonstrate my devotion today?

March 25

SOLEMNITY OF THE ANNUNCIATION

Hail, full of grace, the Lord is with you!

—Luke 1:28

This is the greeting of the Archangel Gabriel to the Blessed Virgin Mary at the Annunciation. Could I be called "full of grace"? How would I respond if a messenger of the Lord came to me?

March 26

---

*Actions speak louder than words. Let your
words teach and your actions speak.*

—From a homily of St. Anthony of Padua

Today, I will be aware of what my words are teaching and what my actions are speaking to others.

March 27

Give up prayer, and you no longer see the inwardness of things; you see only the surface. And with nothing to go by but effects, statistics, and evidence supplied by natural perceptions, you arrive at the wrong conclusions.

—Dom Hubert van Zeller, *Holiness for Housewives*

How many wrong conclusions have I arrived at because I did not pray? Lord, give me the steadfastness of heart to seek You in all things, to adore You through all things, to love You above all things. Amen.

March 28

✳

We know we have souls. But we seldom consider the precious things that can be found in this soul, or who dwells within it, or its high value. Consequently, little effort is made to preserve its beauty. All our attention is taken up with the plainness of the diamond's setting . . . that is, with these bodies of ours.

—St. Teresa of Ávila, *The Interior Castle*

✳

What one thing can I do today specifically to preserve the beauty of my soul?

March 29

Most cradle Catholics have gone through, or need to go through, a second conversion which binds them with a more mature love and obedience to the Church.

—Dorothy Day, "Reflections During Advent, Part Four: Obedience"

Why is this statement true? Does it apply to me?

March 30

In three different ways, woman can fulfill the mission of motherliness: in marriage, in the practice of a profession that values human development, and under the veil as the spouse of Christ.

—St. Teresa Benedicta of the Cross
(Edith Stein), *Essays on Woman*

Which way has God selected for me to fulfill my mission of motherliness? How am I cooperating with His grace?

March 31

It is not wrong to want to live better; what is wrong is a style of life which is presumed to be better when it is directed toward "having" rather than "being."

—Pope St. John Paul II, *Centisimus Annus*, 36

What do I consider the essentials I need to make my life better? How can I redirect these according to the insight of Pope St. John Paul II?

Chapter Four

Meditations

FOR

APRIL

April 1

For Christ also died for sins once for all, the righteous
for the unrighteous, that he might bring us to God.

—1 Peter 3:18

What have been some key moments in my life through which Christ was leading me on the road of salvation? What can I do today to show Him my appreciation?

April 2

*When we were baptized into Christ and
clothed ourselves in Him, we were transformed
into the likeness of the Son of God.*

—St. Cyril of Jerusalem, *Catechetical Lectures*

Of all the people I know, who most images the Son of God to me? How is the "likeness of the Son of God" seen in me?

April 3

---

*Although he was a Son, he learned obedience through
what he suffered; and being made perfect he became
the source of eternal salvation to all who obey him.*

—Hebrews 5:8–9

Obedience led Jesus to the Cross. To what extent am I willing to obey Jesus and His Church even if it should lead to suffering?

April 4

None of us lives to himself, and none of us dies to himself.

—Romans 14:7

How does our contemporary society show contempt for this verse from Sacred Scripture? To what extent do I personally do the same?

April 5

ST. VINCENT FERRER (1350–1419)

You must open the interior eyes of your soul on this light, on this heaven within you, a vast horizon stretching far beyond the realm of human activity.

—From a letter of St. Vincent Ferrer

How "open" are my spiritual eyes to the heaven within me? What adjustments can I make, both interior and exterior, to perceive more clearly the life of God within me?

April 6

However severe God's guidance may seem to us at times, it's always the guidance of a Father who is infinitely good, wise, and kind.

—Traditionally attributed to St. Julie Billiart

Recall a time when you experienced the truth of this quote. How did God's guidance seem to be severe but prove to be good, wise, and kind? Make a mental note to remember this the next time a trial comes your way.

April 7

ST. JEAN-BAPTISTE DE LA SALLE (1651–1719)

Adapt yourself with gracious and charitable compliance to all your neighbor's weaknesses. In particular, make a rule to hide your feelings in many inconsequential matters.

—St. Jean-Baptiste de la Salle to his Christian Brothers

How is God speaking to me—right this moment—through this quote? What is my response?

THE LIFE OF ST. JEAN-BAPTISTE DE LA SALLE

Jean-Baptiste de la Salle was born in Reims, France, in 1651. His father desired his eldest son to follow him in the practice of law, but by the age of eleven Jean-Baptiste had already received the tonsure—a shaving of the top of the head—that was a first step in preparation for clerical life. By sixteen he was living at Reims Cathedral, and in 1678 he was ordained to the priesthood.

Shortly after his ordination, de la Salle became chaplain and confessor for the recently formed Sisters of the Child Jesus, whose mission was to care for and educate poor girls. He soon helped the sisters found a school in Reims, and in the process he discovered his passion for education. Through education, de la Salle believed, he could improve the station of the poor in this world and the next.

In order to help the struggling teachers of Reims, de la Salle would have them to his family's opulent home for meals, and soon he had invited several to live with him. His outreach scandalized his family and his class, and he soon lost the house; shortly thereafter, de la Salle gave all his inheritance to the poor suffering from famine in northeast France.

To further his passion for education, de la Salle founded the Institute of the Brothers of the Christian Schools, known in the United States as the Christian Brothers. St. Jean-Baptiste focused on training his lay brothers to be effective teachers of all children, especially the poor; he founded what is believed to be the first school specifically to train teachers. His institute soon spread around the world, and today there are more than one million students in Lasallian institutions.

April 8

Of all the movements, sensations and feelings of the soul, love is the only one in which the creature can respond to the Creator and make some sort of similar return however unequal though it be.

—From a sermon of St. Bernard

What realities about love are implicit in this statement by St. Bernard?

April 9

Love has a hem to her garment
That reaches the very dust.
It sweeps the stains
From the streets and lanes,
And because it can, it must.

—Anonymous poem, beloved by St.
Teresa of Calcutta, describing St. Fabiola

How dusty has my hem gotten in service of others?

April 10

*The great truth that God is all, and the rest nothing, becomes
the life of the soul, and upon it one can lean securely
amid the incomprehensible mysteries of this world.*

—Traditionally attributed to Bl. Mary Teresa De Soubiran

What current "incomprehensible mystery" draws me to lean on the truth that "God is all and the rest nothing"? What consolation does this give me?

April 11

ST. STANISLAUS, BISHOP AND MARTYR (1030–1097)

The blood of martyrs is the seed of Christians.

—A maxim of Tertullian

What one mortification can I perform today for the sake of the Church that I may be more in union with the martyrs?

April 12

When we really love, we rejoice in the
happiness of the loved one and make
every sacrifice to procure it for him.

—St. Thérèse of Lisieux, *Story of a Soul*

According to this quote, how much do I really love?

April 13

Mary, Queen of Peace, is close to the women of our
day because of her motherhood, her example of openness
to others' needs, and her witness of suffering.

—From an address of Pope St. John
Paul II, "Women: Teachers of Peace"

How can I seek the example, wisdom, and intercession of the
Blessed Mother today to make me a "teacher of peace?"

April 14

*How often I have failed in my duty to God, because
I was not leaning on the strong pillar of prayer.*

—St. Teresa of Ávila, her *Life* (paraphrase)

Is this my lament, too? What resolution am I willing to make?

April 15

Our Lady is rest for those who work, consolation for those who weep, medicine for the sick, a harbor for those assailed by tempests, pardon for sinners, sweet relief for the sad, succor for those who implore.

—St. John Damascene, *Homily on Our Lady's Dormition*

Who is the Blessed Mother to me today? How am I experiencing her maternal love?

BLESSINGS IN THE CHECKOUT LINE

I recently met a young man named Denny and was immediately smitten. It didn't matter that he was forty years my junior; from the moment he flashed that toothy grin and asked, "How are you tonight, young lady?" my heart was captured.

It was clear that Denny both enjoyed his job and the people he met while doing it. He bagged my groceries with the precision of an engineer and the banter of a 1940s leading man.

But what made Denny truly special was his guileless demeanor. He was sincere—even in calling me a "young lady."

Some would say that Denny is challenged. I would say he is challenging.

He challenged me to find pleasure in the mundane. He challenged me to embrace a smile and give one back. He challenged me to find joy in the most unlikely places.

He challenged me to strive for authenticity and generosity of spirit. He challenged me to remember that every human person is a child of God imprinted with His image and likeness.

And finally, Denny challenged me to be kind, courteous, sincere, and unassuming.

After he handed me my bags, I heard Denny greet the next customer in line, "And how are you this evening? Hope it's being good to you!" With a smile and a tear I walked to my car enriched and blessed.

We need more Dennys—people who remind us that we are called to be the very presence of God in the midst of our everyday circumstances and situations. I'm willing to try to be a "Denny." Are you?

April 16

Faith: avoid defeatism and sterile lamenting about the religious situation of your countries, and get on with the job with effort and move . . . many people. Hope: God does not lose battles.

—St. Josemaría Escrivá, paraphrase reported in *In Conversation with God*, Volume 2, by Francis Fernandez

---

According to St. Josemaría, how can I exhibit faith and hope about the religious situation of my country?

April 17

He who is faithful in a very little is faithful also in much.

—Luke 16:10

What "very little" has been entrusted to me? What can I do to ensure that God will also entrust much more to me?

April 18

If you know how to speak without wounding, although you may have to correct or reprimand, hearts will not close themselves to you. The seed will fall on truly fertile ground and the harvest will be plentiful.

—Fr. Salvatore Canals, *Jesus as Friend*

This word is meant just for me today. What strategy can I employ to heed its advice?

April 19

*The soul truly in love with God never fails through laziness
to do all in its power to seek God's Son, the Beloved.*

—St. John of the Cross, *The Spiritual Canticle*

What is within my power to do today "to seek God's Son,
the Beloved"?

April 20

Ceasing to struggle because of our defects when there is opposition to a serious mistake can lead us to that form of pride called pusillanimity, lack of courage and strength to bear misfortune or undertake large enterprises.

—Francis Fernandez, *In Conversation with God*, Volume 2

Am I being tempted in this way today? Regarding what? How can I overcome this temptation?

April 21

ST. ANSELM, BISHOP AND DOCTOR (1033–1109)

O God, let me know you and love you so that I may find my joy in you; and if I cannot do so fully in this life, let me at least make some progress every day, until at last that knowledge, love and joy come to me in all their plentitude.

—A prayer of St. Anselm

Today I will look "at least [to] make some progress" to find all my joy in God, Who gave me life. St. Anselm, pray for me.

THE LIFE OF ST. ANSELM

*T*he *Oxford Dictionary of the Christian Church* calls St. Anselm "the most luminous and penetrating intellect between St. Augustine and St. Thomas Aquinas." He is considered one of the innovators of Scholasticism, the mode of philosophical and theological analysis that dominates Catholic intellectual life to this day.

But perhaps most amazingly of all, while Anselm was writing dozens of the most enduring philosophical and theological works of his era, he was also participating in — and winning — high-stakes political and ecclesiastical battles. This was, however, not the life he had expected, or even wanted for himself.

Born around the year 1033 in what is now far northwest Italy, from an early age Anselm wanted to live the contemplative life of a monk or hermit. At the age of twenty-seven he entered the Benedictine Abbey at Bec in northeast France. Within only a few years he became the prior of the abbey, and in 1078 he was elected abbot; during this time Bec became one of the great centers of intellectual life in Europe.

Upon the death of the Archbishop of Canterbury—Anselm's friend Lafranc—in 1089, Anselm was widely expected to be named to the most important Church post in England. But this was the time of the Investiture Controversy, when the Church was trying to assert her exclusive right to appoint bishops, independent of secular rulers. Anselm did not accept his appointment until he received assurances from King William II about the independence of the Church.

From 1093 until his death in 1109, Anselm did battle with two English kings and was twice exiled for defending the Church's rights in ecclesiastical affairs. By the time of his death, after constant and courageous struggle, Anselm had implemented the Gregorian Reform in England and secured the Church's independence from the king.

April 22

*Lord, give me the heart of a child, and the
awesome courage to live it out as an adult.*

—Catherine de Hueck Doherty, *Molchanie*

What characterizes the heart of a child? Of these traits, which one do I most need to acquire? At this moment, I will ask God for the grace to develop this attribute.

April 23

ST. GEORGE, MARTYR (280–303)

As for Saint George, he was consumed with the fire of the Holy Spirit. Armed with the invincible standard of the cross, he did battle with an evil king and acquitted himself so well that, in vanquishing the king, he overcame the prince of all wicked spirits, and encouraged other soldiers of Christ to perform brave deeds in his cause.

—From a homily of St. Peter Damian on St. George

Could I be called "St. Georgette" today? In what way do I emulate St. George?

April 24

ST. FIDELIS, PRIEST
AND MARTYR (1577–1622)

In addition to this charity, he was faithful in truth as
well as in name. His zeal for defending the Catholic
faith was unsurpassed and he preached it tirelessly.

—From a eulogy for St. Fidelis

We need more people like St. Fidelis in our midst today. Given the circumstances of my life, how can I respond to this need?

April 25

ST. MARK, EVANGELIST

---

*The Church, which has spread everywhere,
even to the ends of the earth, received the faith
from the apostles and their disciples.*

—St. Irenaeus, *Against Heresies*

Dear St. Mark, thank you for your faithfulness to the movement of the Holy Spirit. Through your obedience, I have received faith. Through your docility, I have received strength. Help me to live the gospel message, experience the gospel message, and pass the gospel message on to others. Please pray for me. Amen.

April 26

Why do you spend your money for that which is not bread, and your labor for that which does not satisfy? Hearken diligently to me, and eat what is good, and delight yourselves in fatness.

—Isaiah 55:2

Is it possible that my "consumerism" prevents me from receiving the spiritual nourishment that I need?

April 27

---

*Every kingdom divided against itself is laid waste, and
no city or house divided against itself will stand.*

—Matthew 12:25

How is this passage speaking to me today regarding family
relationships, business relationships, friendships, or community activities?

April 28
ST. LOUIS DE MONTFORT (1673–1716)

*The greatest saints, the souls richest in graces and virtues,
shall be the most assiduous in praying to our Blessed
Lady, and in having her always present as their perfect
model for imitation and their powerful aid for help.*

—St. Louis de Montfort, *True Devotion to Mary*

According to St. Louis de Montfort, how rich in grace and virtue might my soul be? To what extent can I increase my devotion to the Blessed Mother and her intercession?

April 29

ST. CATHERINE OF SIENA (1347–1380)

Eternal Trinity, Godhead, You could give me no greater gift than the gift of Yourself. For You are a fire ever burning and never consumed, which itself consumes all the selfish love that fills my being. Yes, You are a fire that takes away coldness, illuminates the mind with its light, and causes me to know Your truth. You are beauty and wisdom itself.

—Adapted from a prayer of St. Catherine of Siena

Today, I will take a few moments to meditate on this prayer of St. Catherine and see what the Lord speaks to me through it.

THE LIFE OF ST. CATHERINE OF SIENA

St. Catherine di Giacomo di Benincasa is one of the six patron saints of Europe. She was born on March 25, 1347, in Siena, a small city in central Italy. It is said that she had her first vision of Jesus, on His throne as ruler of the world, at the age of five or six. And at seven years old she consecrated herself to the Lord.

Like so many saints, Catherine resisted her family's attempts to dissuade her from total commitment to religious life. When she was asked to marry her elder sister's widower, she fasted until they relented. When her mother insisted that she beautify herself to attract a husband, she cut off her hair.

As a young woman, Catherine experienced a vision of St. Dominic, which encouraged her to join the Dominican tertiaries—women who took the Dominican habit and committed to a life of prayer but did not live in community. Even so, she largely retired from public interactions until she experienced a "mystical marriage" with Jesus, which led to her reemergence in society, helping the poor and attracting followers by her natural charisma.

Catherine put this charisma to use by traveling around Italy advocating for causes such as the reform of the clergy and the return of the papacy from Avignon to Rome. Her appearances and letters continued to grow her reputation around Europe, and soon she became a trusted adviser to popes and other churchmen—an unprecedented role for a woman in the fourteenth century.

In the end, St. Catherine's incredible regimen of mortification, especially with regard to food, hampered her health. She died in Rome in 1380 at the age of thirty-three.

April 30

FEAST OF ST. PIUS V (1504–1572)

O Lord, increase my sufferings and my patience.

—Dying words of St. Pius V

Do I have the courage to pray this prayer? Why or why not? What virtue do I most need to acquire to do so?

Chapter Five

Meditations

FOR

MAY

May 1
FEAST OF ST. JOSEPH THE WORKER

St. Joseph is the best protector to help you in your life, to penetrate the spirit of the Gospel. Indeed, from the Heart of the God-Man, Savior of the world, this spirit is infused in you and in all men, but it is certain that there was no worker's spirit so perfectly and deeply penetrated as the putative father of Jesus, who lived with him in the closest intimacy and community of family and work. So, if you want to be close to Christ, I repeat to you "Ite ad Ioseph": Go to Joseph!

—*From an address of Pope Pius XII to Italian workers*

How are my labor and my leisure fruitful for my salvation and that of others? What can I do in each to make them more so? How can St. Joseph's example and intercession aid me to do so?

May 2
ST. ATHANASIUS (296–373)

He who confesses his sins freely receives pardon
from the priest by virtue of the grace of Christ.

—St. Athanasius, *Fragments Against Novatian* (paraphrase)

What most holds me back from confessing my sins "freely" to the priest who hears my confession in the person of Jesus? Am I willing to bring this defect to the sacrament for healing?

May 3

STS. PHILIP AND JAMES, APOSTLES

How great a forest is set ablaze by a small fire! And the tongue is a fire. The tongue is an unrighteous world among our members, staining the whole body, setting on fire the cycle of nature.

—James 3:5–6

Have I started "fires" of gossip among my friends and family by failing to control my tongue? I will resolve to consider my words more deeply, for my sake and others'.

NO ONE CAN MAKE YOU HAPPY

Joy arises in us when our will possesses some desirable good that leads to authentic happiness."

I recently came across this sentence in an old Catholic periodical, and it got me thinking about how no one and, in the end, no physical thing can make us happy. Authentic happiness derives from possessing the ultimate good.

The ultimate good must be, of course, perfection itself, and there is only one true perfection: God. God is Ultimate Goodness, and therefore all else that is good proceeds from Him. The personification of this goodness is Jesus Christ. Therefore, anything that leads us to Christ is good because in being led to Christ we are led to God. In Psalm 37:4 we read, "Take delight in the LORD, and he will give you the desires of your heart." Well, the one fundamental desire of the human heart is happiness. But what does it mean to "take delight in the Lord"?

We delight in Him by knowing Him, loving Him, and serving Him. In other words, we delight in Him through divine intimacy—union with Him. Only God possessing us—and we possessing Him—can bring us happiness. Where do I go to find my happiness? Do I believe my happiness is dependent on others or on the attainment of possessions, titles, and prestige?

Do the things that I desire lead me closer to God or further from Him?

Answering these questions requires fortitude, honesty, and self-knowledge. But if we are truly seeking ultimate happiness —the perfection of joy—we must constantly examine our words, our actions, and our desires.

May 4

Do not be dismayed, daughters, at the number of things which you have to consider before setting out on this Divine journey, which is the royal road to Heaven. . . . Let us now return to those who wish to travel on this road, and will not halt until they reach their goal. . . . It is most important . . . that they should begin well by making an earnest and most determined resolve not to halt until they reach their goal, whatever may come, whatever may happen to them, however hard they may have to labor, whoever may complain of them, whether they reach their goal or die on the road.

—St. Teresa of Ávila, *The Way of Perfection*

According to this quote, do I really want to be a saint? What worry, fear, or concern crosses my mind when I read St. Teresa's "saintly standard"? Am I willing to say, "Jesus, I trust in You" in this area?

May 5

A rock pile ceases to be a rock pile the
moment a single man contemplates it, bearing
within him the image of a cathedral.

—Antoine de Saint-Exupéry, *Flight to Arras*

What "rock pile" is currently facing me? What "cathedral"
may lie within it?

May 6

The splendor of the rose and the whiteness of the lily do not rob the little violet of its scent nor the daisy of its simple charm. I realized that if every tiny flower wanted to be a rose, spring would lose its loveliness and there would be no wild flowers to make the meadows gay.

—St. Thérèse of Lisieux, *Story of a Soul*

Is there someone of whom I am envious or jealous? To what extent does this quote help me praise God for his or her gift? What gift do I have that makes me a flower in the garden of life?

May 7

The gate of heaven is very low;
only the humble can enter it.

—From the writings of St. Elizabeth Ann Seton

What is one thing that makes me too tall to enter the gate of heaven? What is another?

May 8

With all things, it is always what comes to us from outside, freely and by surprise as a gift from heaven, without our having sought it, that brings us pure joy.

—Simone Weil, *Gravity and Grace*

Today, I will seek at least one instance of "pure joy" in my daily life, and I will reflect on it in my time of prayer.

May 9

ST. PACHOMIUS (CA. 292–346)

Though abstinence and prayer be of great merit, yet sickness, suffered with patience, is of much greater.

—St. Pachomius, recorded in
Lives of the Saints by Fr. Alban Butler

In my current sickness or suffering, how can I exercise patience for the love of God so that it can be redemptive for me and for others?

May 10
ST. DAMIEN OF MOLOKAI (1840–1889)

Unite your heart with God. And especially, in the midst of temptation, protest ceaselessly that you prefer to die instantly rather than consent to the least venial sin.

—From the "Personal Rule" of St. Damien of Molokai

What is my most common temptation? How can I "protest ceaselessly" against it?

May 11

*A mere smile, a short visit, the lighting of a lamp, writing
a letter for a blind man, carrying a bucket of charcoal,
reading the newspaper for someone — something small,
very small — may, in fact, be our love of God in action.*

—St. Teresa of Calcutta, *In the Heart of the World*

How did I show "love of God in action" yesterday? In what small way will I resolve to show my "love of God in action" today?

THE LIFE OF ST. DAMIEN
OF MOLOKAI

Captain James Cook, a British explorer, was the first known European to set foot on the Hawaiian Islands in 1779. Once the islands were on European maps, new residents flowed to the islands, bringing diseases to which the native Hawaiians had no immunity. Among those diseases was leprosy.

Meanwhile, Jozef de Veuster was born in 1840 in Belgium. His father intended him to follow in his own career as a merchant, but young Jozef was drawn to the religious life and entered the novitiate of the Congregation of the Sacred Hearts of Jesus and Mary in 1858. He took the religious name Damien and prayed daily to be sent on a mission. Six years later, in 1864, he got his wish; Damien was ordained a priest in Honolulu, Hawaii, in May 1864.

At that time leprosy was considered to be a highly contagious and incurable disease, so a year after Fr. Damien's ordination, the government of the Kingdom of Hawaii set up a quarantine facility for lepers on the isolated north coast of the island of Molokai. The government could afford to house and feed the residents of the quarantine, but not to provide effective medical and palliative care. So, in 1873, Fr. Damien volunteered to serve them.

For sixteen years, Fr. Damien lived among the lepers of Molokai, administering the sacraments, dressing the lepers' wounds, building their cottages, fashioning their coffins, and digging their graves. In 1884 he contracted leprosy himself, and on April 15, 1889, he died from the disease. The entire population of the quarantine participated in his funeral.

May 12

STS. NEREUS AND ACHILLEUS, ST. PANCRAS, MARTYRS (FIRST CENTURY)

The believer who has seriously pondered his Christian vocation, including what Revelation has to say about the possibility of martyrdom, cannot exclude it from his own life's horizon. The two thousand years since the birth of Christ are marked by the ever-present witness of the martyrs.

—Pope John Paul II, *Incarnationis Mysterium*

Should circumstances require it, am I willing to suffer martyrdom for the sake of the Church?

May 13
OUR LADY OF FÁTIMA

You have seen hell where the souls of sinners go. To save them God wishes to establish in the world devotion to my Immaculate Heart. If you do what I tell you many souls will be saved and there will be peace.

—The Blessed Mother to Lucy, Jacinta, and Francisco

In what one way can I help to spread devotion to the Immaculate Heart of Mary?

May 14

ST. MATTHIAS, APOSTLE

*Lord, who knowest the hearts of all men, show
which one of these two thou hast chosen.*

—Acts: 1:24

How willing am I to surrender all of my choices to the will of God? In what one way can I begin today to grow in this virtue?

May 15

ST. DYMPHNA, VIRGIN AND MARTYR (D. CA. 620)

Hear us, O God, Our Savior! You chose St. Dymphna as heavenly patron of those afflicted with mental and emotional illness. Through her prayers grant relief and consolation to all who suffer in this way. . . . Through the intercession of St. Dymphna, graciously grant those for whom we pray patience in suffering and resignation to your divine will. We ask this through Christ, Our Lord. Amen.

—Traditional prayer for the intercession of St. Dymphna

For whom do I need to ask St. Dymphna's intercession? I resolve to use this prayer to pray for him or her for the next week or more as the Holy Spirit leads me.

THE LIFE OF ST. DYMPHNA

Although she is said to have lived in the seventh century, St. Dymphna didn't come into Church tradition until the thirteenth century, when her legend was first recorded. The story of her life is said to have been passed down in oral tradition, and many healings of the mentally ill are attributed to her intercession.

The traditional story is that Dymphna was the daughter of a minor Irish king, Damon, a pagan. Dymphna's mother (and Damon's wife), however, was a Christian, and so the young girl was brought up in Christianity. It is said that as a teenager, Dymphna consecrated herself to Christ.

Around this time, her mother died, plunging Damon into despair that deepened into severe mental illness. He finally agreed to remarry but sought only a woman as beautiful as his wife had been. Soon, he turned his attention to the woman who most resembled her: Dymphna.

In order to uphold her vow, Dymphna fled the kingdom along with her priest, crossing the sea to Belgium. It is said that in Geel, she used her family's wealth to set up a home for the sick and the marginalized, but soon her father caught up with her. Enraged by her resistance, he killed his daughter and the priest.

Upon the apparent discovery of her tomb in the Middle Ages, pilgrims swarmed to Geel to seek healing, and it is said that many were cured of serious mental illness. St. Dymphna's legacy lives on not just in her patronage of those suffering from psychological troubles, but in Geel itself, which remains an international center of innovation in the humane care of the mentally ill.

May 16

I travel, work, suffer my weak health, meet with a thousand difficulties, but all these are nothing, for this world is so small. To me, space is an imperceptible object, as I am accustomed to dwell in eternity.

—Traditionally attributed to St. Frances Cabrini

Is my perception earthly bound or eternally bound?

May 17

It is not enough for Christian parents to nourish only the bodies of their children; even animals do this. They must also nourish their souls in grace, in virtue, and in God's holy commandments.

—Traditionally attributed to St. Catherine of Siena

In light of natural motherhood and spiritual motherhood, what can I do to nourish better those entrusted to me "in grace, in virtue, and God's holy commandments"?

May 18

FEAST OF ST. JOHN I, POPE
AND MARTYR (470–526)

───────────── ✳ ─────────────

*From the psychological point of view, martyrdom is the most
eloquent proof of the truth of the faith, for faith can give a
human face even to the most violent of deaths and show its
beauty even in the midst of the most atrocious persecutions.*

—Pope John Paul II, *Incarnationis Mysterium*

───────────── ✳ ─────────────

Today, I will consider the depth of the martyr's love of God
and beg for the grace to love Him as much.

May 19

*Fight all error, but do it with good humor, patience,
kindness, and love. Harshness will damage
your own soul and spoil the best cause.*

—St. John of Kanty to his students

To what extent do the virtues of good humor, patience,
kindness, and love accompany my efforts to expose error?
What one strategy can I employ to guard against harshness?

May 20

Christ is now exalted above the heavens, but He still suffers on earth all the pain that we, the members of His body, have to bear. . . . Why do we on earth not strive to find rest with Him in heaven even now, through the faith, hope and love that unites us to Him?

—From a sermon of St. Augustine

Today I resolve to spend at least fifteen minutes in quiet meditation so that I may be united to Jesus in Heaven through faith, hope, and love.

May 21

If you're a Catholic you believe what the Church teaches and the climate makes no difference.

—From a letter of Flannery O'Connor

Am I a Catholic? Or do I let the ebb and flow of trends and fashions shape my beliefs?

May 22

ST. RITA OF CASCIA (1377–1457)

Remain in the holy love of Jesus. Remain in obedience to the holy Roman Church. Remain in peace and fraternal charity.

—Reported last words of St. Rita of Cascia

Love, obedience, peace, and charity. How can I bring these qualities into my life in some small way today?

May 23

While you are proclaiming peace with your lips, be careful to have it even more fully in your heart.

—Traditionally attributed to St. Francis of Assisi

What has the potential of robbing me of my peace today? What can I do to overcome this temptation?

May 24

---

*Apart from the cross there is no other ladder
by which we may get to heaven.*

—Quoted in a life of St. Rose of Lima

How is God asking me to currently climb this ladder? What is my response?

May 25

ST. MARY MAGDALENE DE PAZZI, VIRGIN (1566–1607)

Those who call to mind the sufferings of Christ, and who offer up their own to God through His passion, find their pains sweet and pleasant.

—St. Mary Magdalene de Pazzi, reported by Fr. Paolo Pirlo in My *First Books of Saints*

What pains or sufferings would God choose to make "sweet and pleasant" for me today? What, then, should I do?

May 26

ST. PHILIP NERI (1515–1595)

Cast yourself with confidence into the arms of God. And be very sure of this, that if He wants anything of you He will fit you for your work and give you strength to do it.

—From an instruction of St. Philip Neri

What is God asking of me today? How should I approach it and why?

May 27

ST. AUGUSTINE OF CANTERBURY (D. CA. 604)

The loving-kindness of Christ has everywhere infused goodwill into preachers of his truth. Thus without thought of themselves they burn with zeal for the salvation of all nations.

—From the message of St. Augustine of Canterbury to King Ethelbert upon arriving in England

---

To what extent do I burn with evangelistic zeal? Today, I resolve to speak of Jesus to one more person than I did yesterday.

THE LIFE OF ST. PHILIP NERI

P hilip Neri was born in Florence in 1515 into a noble family of civil servants. At the age of eighteen he underwent a profound religious conversion, no longer showing interest in his family's wealth or prestige; it is said that he tore up a document proving his family's noble lineage. He then moved to Rome, where he soon earned the name "the Apostle of Rome."

He studied and served the poor for many years in Rome, including by founding a lay apostolate called the Confraternity of the Holy Trinity, which ministered to the thousands of often-poor pilgrims who came to the city. Then in 1551, at the age of thirty-six, Neri was ordained a priest.

Fr. Neri's priestly life was marked by an incredible dedication to the sacraments, especially confession and adoration of the Blessed Sacrament. He spent much of his time in the confessional, hearing dozens, even hundreds of confessions per day.

The saint soon gathered around himself a group of men, young and old, with whom he met regularly to pray, to sing, and to discuss matters of faith. Out of these gatherings developed the first oratory, or house of prayer, under Fr. Neri's leadership. By 1575, the Congregation of the Oratory had been fully approved by Rome.

Fr. Neri's congregation was the most democratically organized religious foundation of its time. Oratorian priests live in community, but they do not take vows and they maintain a high degree of independence, as does each oratory. This corresponds to St. Philip's personal spirituality, which focused on individual piety, good cheer, and public outreach.

St. Philip Neri died after a day of hearing confessions in late May 1595.

May 28

God is closer to us than water is to a fish.

—St. Catherine of Siena, *Dialogue* (paraphrase)

How can God be closer to me than water is to a fish? What means can I employ to help me experience His very close presence?

May 29

I found Him when I took leave of all creatures. I found Him in my inmost heart. When I am silent with men I am able to converse with God and with Him I always find perfect peace.

—Br. Lawrence of the Resurrection,
The Practice of the Presence of God

What three steps does Brother Lawrence recommend we employ to find God? What must I do or do differently to incorporate these steps into my everyday life?

May 30

Nothing is far from God.

—Quoted in a life of St. Monica

What one intention today do I desire to be very near to God? How do these words of St. Monica give me hope and consolation?

May 31

FEAST OF THE VISITATION OF MARY

*And blessed is she who believed that there would be a
fulfilment of what was spoken to her from the Lord.*

—Luke 1:45

To what extent do I believe that God's word to me will be
fulfilled? What can I do to increase my trust?

Chapter Six

Meditations

FOR

JUNE

June 1

ST. JUSTIN MARTYR (CA. 100–165)

*The food that has been made the Eucharist by
the prayer of His Word, and which nourishes our
flesh and blood by assimilation, is both the Flesh
and Blood of that Jesus Who was made flesh.*

—St. Justin Martyr, *First Apology*

When have I experienced or witnessed the healing effects
of the Eucharist—physically or spiritually?

June 2

SAINTS MARCELLINUS AND
PETER, MARTYRS (D. CA. 304)

*We should be extremely eager to share in
Christ's sufferings and to let them be multiplied
in us if we desire the superabundant consolation
that will be given those who mourn.*

—Origen, *Exhortation to Martyrdom*

What is the form of my "martyrdom" right now? How is
God consoling me in the midst of it?

June 3

ST. CHARLES LWANGA AND COMPANIONS, MARTYRS (D. 1886)

These African martyrs herald the dawn of a new age. If only the mind of man might be directed not toward persecutions and religious conflicts but toward a rebirth of Christianity and civilization!

—From the homily of Pope Paul VI at the canonization of St. Charles Lwanga and Companions

To what extent is my mind directed toward a rebirth of Christianity and civilization? What should I do about it?

June 4

Prayer is to our soul what rain is to the soil.
Fertilize the soil ever so richly; it will remain
barren unless fed by frequent rains.

—Traditionally attributed to St. John Vianney

Is the soil of my soul moist and rich or dry and arid?

June 5

ST. BONIFACE, BISHOP AND MARTYR (673–754)

*Let us preach the whole of God's plan to the
powerful and to the humble, to rich and to poor,
to men of every rank and age, as far as God gives
us strength, in season and out of season.*

—Traditionally attributed to a homily of St. Boniface

To what extent do I preach the whole of God's plan, or to what extent do I water down His message?

June 6

TRINITY SUNDAY

*We worship one God in Trinity, and Trinity in Unity;
Neither confounding the Persons; nor dividing the Essence.
For there is one Person of the Father; another of the Son;
and another of the Holy Ghost. But the Godhead of the
Father, of the Son, and of the Holy Ghost, is all one; the
Glory equal, the Majesty coeternal. Such as the Father
is; such is the Son; and such is the Holy Ghost.*

—From the Creed of St. Athanasius

Although it is impossible to comprehend the mystery of the Trinity with our intellect, we can experience relationship with the Trinity in our soul. To what extent can I attest to this truth?

June 7

All high and glorious God,
Cast Your light into the darkness of my heart.
Give me right faith, perfect charity, and a profound humility,
With wisdom and perception, O Lord, that I might know
And do what is truly Your holy and perfect will. Amen.

—Prayer of St. Francis of Assisi

Which attribute in this prayer do I most need today? I will now ask God, in my own words, to grace me with it for His honor and glory.

June 8

Take from the "Mother of mercy" and "Consolation of the afflicted" an example and inspiration at every moment. She will guide you to her Son and will teach you the value of every soul.

—From an address of Pope St. John
Paul II to the Mercedarians

How has Mary aided me under both of the titles mentioned in today's quote? Currently, what one soul is she showing me the value of?

June 9
ST. EPHREM (306–373)

Savior, Your divine plan for the world is a mirror for the spiritual world; teach us to walk in that world as spiritual men.

—From a homily of St. Ephrem

In what one way is Jesus asking me to walk in the spirit rather than in the flesh? Is there an obstacle to doing so? How can I overcome it?

GOLDEN APPLES AND
SILVER SETTINGS

Some years ago I overheard a father calmly reprimanding his child. What struck me about the conversation was the dad's choice of words, his gentle tone of voice, and his loving disposition. It was clear that in the midst of the admonition this father was communicating love, encouragement, and hope.

As the conversation came to a close with a loving hug, I began to think about the creative power of words. It was clear to me that the words this father had spoken were powerful and would have a positive impact on his little boy.

Throughout the first creation account, we see God bringing the world into being through His speech.

But when God creates man, He says, "Let us make man in our image, after our likeness." If we are made in God's image and likeness, and if God creates by speaking, then the words we speak create as well. Like the words of God, our words have creative power.

But unlike God, we are stained by original sin. Our words can be constructive or destructive. Our words can bring comfort, hope, and life — or they can bring anguish, devastation, and death. My favorite Scripture verse on speech is Proverbs 25:11: "A word fitly spoken is like apples of gold in a setting of silver." That father's words to his son were golden apples bringing nourishment to his son's soul and spirit, placed on the silver setting of love and tenderness. So, too, our words must be tempered with the love of God. Then, even in the midst of a reprimand or correction, we will still create "golden apples."

June 10

Nothing is so characteristically Christian as being a peacemaker, and for this reason our Lord has promised us peacemakers a very high reward.

—From a letter of St. Basil the Great

In what one situation am I being called to be a peacemaker (think of all the ways one brings peace)? What three steps can I take to respond to this call?

June 11

ST. BARNABAS

It was clear through unlearned men that the cross was persuasive, in fact, it persuaded the whole world.

—From a commentary of St. John Chrysostom on 1 Corinthians

Holy Apostles and evangelizers of the early Church: Pray for me that I might have the courage and the holy zeal to preach the Gospel when it is convenient and when it is not. May I be inspired by your example today and always. Amen.

June 12

Having confidence in you, O Mother of God, I shall be saved. Being under your protection, I shall fear nothing. With your help I shall give battle to my enemies and put them to flight; for devotion to you is an arm of salvation.

—St. John Damascene, *Homily on Our Lady's Dormition*

How is it that the Blessed Mother protects us and helps us put our enemies to flight? Why is she an "arm of salvation"? Is my devotion to her commensurate with her great mission?

June 13
CORPUS CHRISTI

And let all take care that no unbaptized person tastes of the Eucharist nor a mouse or other animal and that none of it at all fall and be lost. For it is the Body of Christ to be eaten by them that believe and not to be lightly thought of.

—St. Hippolytus, *The Apostolic Tradition*

Does my demeanor toward the Eucharist reflect that I do not think of it lightly? In what one way can I improve my attitude?

June 14

I need to love you more and more, but I don't have any more love in my heart. I have given all my love to you. If you want more, fill my heart with your love.

—From a prayer of St. Padre Pio of Pietrelcina

Am I ready for a "refill" of God's love? How do I know if I am or if I'm not?

June 15

Fathers and mothers owe four things to their children: maintenance, instruction, correction, and good example.

—Traditionally attributed to St. Jean-Baptiste de la Salle

To what extent is my "parental bank account" in the black or in the red according to St. Jean-Baptiste de la Salle? Where might I be coming up short?

June 16

*God bestows more consideration on the purity
of the intention with which our actions are
performed than on the actions themselves.*

—Traditionally attributed to St. Augustine

Today I resolve to do my examination of conscience based on my motivations for my actions. How pure are my intentions?

June 17

The bread that you store up belongs to the hungry, the cloak that lies in your chest belongs to the naked; the gold that you have hidden in the ground belongs to the poor.

—From a homily of St. Basil the Great (paraphrase)

To what extent do I have the food, clothing, and money of others in my possession? What do I resolve to do about it?

June 18

SACRED HEART OF JESUS

All ye who seek a comfort sure
In trouble and distress,
Whatever sorrow vex the mind,
Or guilt the soul oppress:

Jesus, Who gave Himself for you
Upon the Cross to die,
Opens to you His Sacred Heart;
O to that heart draw nigh.

—Anonymous (eighteenth century)

Today, I will consider the one situation or circumstance that is drawing me near to the Sacred Heart. Am I willing to enter that Heart to see what the Lord has in store for me through this situation or circumstance? Why or why not?

June 19

IMMACULATE HEART OF MARY

Fount of love, forever flowing,
With a burning ardor glowing,
Make me, Mother, feel like thee;
Let my heart with grace gifted
All on fire, to Christ be lifted,
And by Him accepted be.

—Traditionally attributed to Jacopone da Todi (thirteenth century)

Which grace of Our Lady's heart does my own heart most emulate? Which one of her graces do I most need to receive? How can I cooperate with that grace?

June 20

Christ does not force our will. He only takes what we give Him. But He does not give Himself entirely until He sees that we yield ourselves entirely to Him.

—St. Teresa of Ávila, *The Way of Perfection*

Today I resolve to spend at least fifteen minutes in quiet meditation asking Jesus to reveal to me what most prevents me from receiving more of Him. And I further resolve, upon this discovery, to surrender this obstacle to Him.

June 21

ST. ALOYSIUS GONZAGA (1568–1591)

There is no more evident sign that anyone is a saint and of the number of the elect than to see him leading a good life and at the same time a prey to desolation, suffering, and trials.

—Traditionally attributed to St. Aloysius Gonzaga

When I am desolate, suffering, or enduring a trial, would my interior and exterior life show that I should be counted among the elect? If not, what needs to be amended?

THE LIFE OF ST. ALOYSIUS GONZAGA

Aloysius (born Luigi; Aloysius is the Latin version of his Italian name) was born into the Gonzaga family, one of the most prominent in northern Italy, on March 9, 1568. He was the eldest son and thus heir to his father's title and his family's military tradition, so at the age of five his father sent him off to military camp.

He continued this training for several years, but during bouts of serious illness he began to pass time in prayer and reading spiritual books. It is reported that he vowed his chastity at age nine. A few years later, after completing service for a Spanish prince, young Aloysius resolved to join the recently formed Jesuit order. But there was a problem: joining the Jesuits would require him to renounce his inheritance and social standing. His parents could not dissuade him, though, and at the age of twenty he entered the novitiate of the Jesuit order.

Six years later, in 1591, and shortly before his planned ordination, an outbreak of plague attacked Rome. Despite his intense revulsion at the sight of plague victims and his own poor health, Aloysius volunteered to serve in the Jesuit hospital. He carried the dying from the streets to the hospital, then cleaned and fed them. After several Jesuits came down with plague, Aloysius's superiors told him to leave the hospital. But he refused, and a compromise was worked out: he would serve the sick in a facility for non–plague victims.

But one patient did have plague, and Aloysius became infected. He died with the name of Jesus on his lips on June 21, 1591, at the age of twenty-three.

June 22

ST. THOMAS MORE (1478–1535)

Do not let your mind be troubled over anything that shall happen to me in this world. Nothing can come but what God wills. And I am very sure that whatever that be, however bad it may seem, it shall indeed be best.

—St. Thomas More to his daughter
during his imprisonment

How have I seen great good be worked out through past suffering? How can this reality help me in my current difficult time?

June 23

The path that leads to holiness is the path of prayer; and prayer ought to take root and grow in the soul little by little, like a tiny seed which later develops into a tree with many branches.

—St. Josemaría Escrivá, *Friends of God*

What one adjustment can I make today to help my prayer life grow a little more? I will pray for the grace to follow through.

THE LIFE OF ST. THOMAS MORE

Thomas More, patron saint of lawyers and politicians, was born in London on February 7, 1478. He attended Oxford University, and by 1502 he was certified as an attorney. He briefly considered entering a Carthusian monastery, but he decided instead to run for Parliament, which he did successfully in 1504.

Unusual for his time, More educated his daughters with the same level of care and sophistication as his son. Other noble families in London took note of this attitude—and the brilliance of his daughters—and adjusted their views toward women's education.

From 1504 onward, Thomas More rose consistently through the English government. Within twenty years he had become a close adviser of King Henry VIII. Meanwhile he wrote important political and legal treatises, most notably *Utopia*, a word and concept that More coined, which (perhaps satirically) offered an example of a perfect society.

In 1527, Henry VIII initiated his famous petition to have his marriage to Catherine of Aragon annulled. Two years later, the king named Thomas More Lord Chancellor, one of the highest royal appointments in the government. More served the king faithfully; he opposed the Protestant Reformation and efficiently arbitrated disputes that came to his office. But More could not support Henry's claim to be the final church authority in England, or his annulment. He resigned in 1532.

When Henry unilaterally divorced Catherine and married Anne Boleyn in 1533, More declined to attend the wedding. This was the last straw for Henry, who had More arrested for treason. When, in the summer of 1535, St. Thomas More refused to sign an oath affirming that the king was the supreme authority in the English church, he was convicted and beheaded. On the scaffold he said, "I die the king's good servant, but God's first."

June 24

NATIVITY OF ST. JOHN THE BAPTIST

*And why is this granted me, that the mother
of my Lord should come to me? For behold,
when the voice of your greeting came to my
ears, the babe in my womb leaped for joy.*

—Luke 1:43–44

Mary carried Jesus in her womb to Zechariah's house, and St. John the Baptist leapt in his mother's womb for joy. Who will carry Jesus to me today, and how will I respond to His presence?

June 25

Our labor here is brief, but our reward is eternal. Be not troubled by the noise of the world that passes like shadow.

—From a letter of St. Clare of Assisi (paraphrase)

Currently, what "noise of the world" is seeking to distract me from my goal of eternal life? In what way can I co-operate with grace to quiet it?

June 26

*If we make a quietness within ourselves, if we silence
all desires and opinions and if with love, without
formulating any words, we bind our whole soul to
think "Thy will be done," the thing which after that
we feel sure we should do . . . is the will of God.*

—Simone Weil, *Gravity and Grace*

In what one area am I presently seeking God's will? According to the quote, what steps should I take to discover it? Am I willing to do so?

June 27

*God's will—peacefully do at each moment
what at the moment ought to be done.*

—Traditionally attributed to St. Katharine Drexel

What ought to be done at this moment of my life?

June 28

ST. IRENAEUS (130–202)

Where there is order, there is also harmony; where there is harmony, there is also correct timing; where there is correct timing, there is also advantage.

—St. Irenaeus, *Against Heresies*

Do I seem to miss my best advantages in prayer, life's circumstances, and personal relationships? According to St. Irenaeus, why might this be? What can I do today to make a change?

June 29

FEASTS OF STS. PETER AND PAUL

There is one day for the passion of two apostles. But these two also were as one; although they suffered on different days, they were as one. Peter went first, Paul followed. We are celebrating a feast day, consecrated for us by the blood of the apostles. Let us love their faith, their lives, their labors, their sufferings, their confession of faith, their preaching.

—From a homily of St. Augustine on
the feast of Sts. Peter and Paul

Today I will witness about Jesus and the Faith to at least one person in union with Sts. Peter and Paul.

June 30

Perform faithfully what God requires of you each moment and leave the thought of everything else to Him. I assure you that to live in this way will bring you great peace.

—Traditionally attributed to St. Jane Frances de Chantal

St. Jane de Chantal gives a secret to the peace-filled life. What are her two recommendations? I will identify the first and pray for the grace to follow through with the second.

Chapter Seven

Meditations

FOR

JULY

July 1

It is most laudable in a married woman to be devout, but she must never forget that she is a housewife and sometimes must leave God at the altar to find Him in her housekeeping.

—St. Frances of Rome recorded in
Lives of the Saints by Fr. Alban Butler

How balanced is my life regarding my duties toward God, family, and career? Do I find God in my daily duties?

July 2

I tell you again and again, my brethren, that in the Lord's garden are to be found not only the roses of His martyrs. In it there are also the lilies of the virgins, the ivy of wedded couples, and the violets of widows.

—From a homily of St. Augustine

Which flower am I in the Lord's garden? How can I better cooperate with the grace of my state in life so that I may eternally bloom before Him?

July 3

ST. THOMAS THE APOSTLE

---

*Unless I see in his hands the print of the nails,
and place my finger in the mark of the nails, and
place my hand in his side, I will not believe.*

—John 20:25

Today and in my present circumstance of life, in what way may I be saying, "I will not believe?" What is the underlying doubt that plagues me?

July 4

One of the greatest disasters that happened to modern civilization was for democracy to inscribe "liberty" on its banners instead of "justice." Because "liberty" was considered the ideal it was not long until some men interpreted it as meaning "freedom from justice."

—Ven. Fulton J. Sheen, "Conditions of a Just War"

How have I seen the truth of Fulton Sheen's observation in contemporary society? What is the Christian response, and how can I give it?

July 5

---

*This is the essential mission of the apostle: to be
a living witness to the greatness and beauty of
Christianity, especially at the present day, when
so many people have concerning religion only false
ideas, prejudices, or total lack of understanding.*

—Fr. Raoul Plus, S.J., *Radiating Christ*

In what three ways will I seek to be a "living witness" today
to the greatness and beauty of Christianity?

July 6
ST. MARIA GORETTI (1890–1902)

Not all of us are expected to die a martyr's death, but we are called to the pursuit of Christian virtue. This demands strength of character . . . a constant, persistent and relentless effort is being asked of us right up to the moment of our death.

—From a homily of Pope Pius XII at the canonization of St. Maria Goretti

Dear Holy Spirit, illuminate for me today the virtue I need to acquire the most. Give me the grace to persist in its achievement today and every day of my life. Amen.

July 7

Mercy imitates God and disappoints Satan.

—Traditionally attributed to St. John Chrysostom

How can I disappoint Satan today?

THE LIFE OF ST. MARIA GORETTI

Maria Goretti was born into a family of farmers in east-central Italy in 1890. When she was still at an early age, poverty forced her family to leave their home and their farm and to travel Italy looking for work—mainly on other, larger farms.

When Maria was nine, the family settled in the Lazio region of Italy, sharing a home with the Serenelli family. Shortly thereafter, her father died of malaria, leaving his wife and six surviving children to support themselves. Maria, the eldest girl, would stay to tend the house and care for the youngest while her mother and other siblings worked in the fields.

The Serenelli family consisted of Giovanni and his son, Alessandro. Many years older than Maria, the troubled young man took an unhealthy interest in her, making advances on multiple occasions. One time, when Maria was home alone with her infant sister, Alessandro threatened her with a knife if she did not permit him to rape her. Maria protested that it would be a mortal sin for him to go through with it, and he stabbed her over a dozen times.

In the hospital, Maria said that she forgave Alessandro and wanted to see him in heaven with her. She died the next day.

Alessandro was arrested for the murder of Maria Goretti and sentenced to thirty years in prison. Three years into his sentence he reported having a vision of Maria, and he repented of his crime. The very day of his release, he sought Maria's mother to ask her forgiveness, which she gave, and they went to Mass together. Alessandro Serenelli later joined the Capuchin order and attended the canonization of his victim in 1950. He died twenty years later.

July 8

One must have lit in oneself so bright a flame of
sympathy and tenderness that all who are beginning as
we are ending can come to find their light and fire.

—Servant of God Elisabeth Leseur,
The Secret Diary of Elisabeth Leseur

Today I will seek two opportunities to ignite in myself the
flame of sympathy and tenderness.

July 9

Be filled with the Spirit, addressing one another in psalms and hymns and spiritual songs . . . always and for everything giving thanks in the name of Jesus Christ to God the Father.

—Ephesians 5:18–19, 20

For what three things can I sing a song of thanksgiving to God the Father today? With whom can I share my hymn of praise?

July 10

*I tell you, there will be more joy in heaven over
one sinner who repents than over ninety-nine
righteous persons who need no repentance.*

—Luke 15:7

For whom should I pray today? What specific prayers and
sacrifices will I make for his or her soul?

July 11

I am concealing Myself from you so that you can discover by yourself what you are without Me.

—Reported words of Our Lord to St. Margaret of Cortona

Does my time of prayer seem dry and arid? Do circumstances appear as though God has abandoned me? Could it be that God is withdrawing His consolations from me so that I may see my utter and total dependence on Him?

July 12

Purity is a precious jewel, and the owner of a precious stone would never dream of making a display of his riches in the presence of thieves.

—Traditionally attributed to St. John Bosco

Considering my dress, my language, my demeanor, and my behavior, to what extent do I make a "display" of my riches?

July 13

The devil is only permitted to tempt thee as much as is profitable for thy exercise and trial, and in order that thou, who didst not know thyself, mayest find out what thou art.

— Traditionally attributed to St. Augustine

How am I currently being tempted? What might the Lord be revealing to me about myself through it? What faithful response will I make?

July 14

FEAST OF SAINT KATERI TEKAKWITHA, "LILY OF THE MOHAWKS," VIRGIN (1656–1680)

Jesus, Mary, I love you.

—Reported last words of St. Kateri Tekakwitha

How can I keep the love of Jesus and His mother Mary in the front of my mind today?

July 15

SAINT BONAVENTURE, BISHOP AND DOCTOR OF THE CHURCH (CA. 1218–1274)

A constant fidelity in small things is a great and heroic virtue.

—St. Bonaventure, recorded in
Lives of the Saints by Fr. Alban Butler

In what small thing is God asking me to exercise "constant fidelity"?

THE LIFE OF ST. KATERI TEKAKWITHA

Given at birth the name Tekakwitha, which means "she who bumps into things," St. Kateri is the first Native American to have been canonized. She was born in 1656 in a Mohawk village in upstate New York. Her father was the village chief, and her mother was an Algonquin Christian who had been baptized by Jesuit missionaries and captured in battle.

At the age of four, Tekakwitha's parents and younger brother died in a smallpox epidemic; the young girl contracted the illness and survived, but her face was permanently scarred. She went to live with extended family and was cared for by them and by the village at large.

Mohawk custom held that young women were to be married in their early teens, and so Tekakwitha's family began pressuring her to marry at age thirteen. She consistently resisted, however, even fleeing the village for a time to avoid her adopted aunt's attempted matchmaking.

Meanwhile, French soldiers and fur traders had swept into Mohawk country, bringing with them Jesuit missionaries. It is said that Tekakwitha loved the Faith from the moment she heard of it, but it took many years for her to gain the confidence to be baptized.

On Easter Sunday, 1676, at the age of nineteen, Tekakwitha was baptized under the patronage of St. Catherine of Siena—in Mohawk, "Kateri." Under threat from other villagers, she moved to a Catholic village and Jesuit mission in present-day Canada, where she adopted a rudimentary habit. She is said to have undertaken great penances and mortifications, earning a reputation for prayerfulness and holiness.

St. Kateri Tekakwitha died in the mission five years later, at the age of twenty-four. It is said that within fifteen minutes of her death, her smallpox scars faded and her face glowed radiantly.

July 16
OUR LADY OF MOUNT CARMEL

O beautiful Flower of Carmel, most fruitful vine,
splendor of heaven, holy and singular, who brought
forth the Son of God, still ever remaining a pure virgin,
assist me in my necessities. O Star of the Sea, help and
protect me. Show me that you are my Mother.

—From a prayer of St. Simon Stock

In what one way would I ask Our Lady to show me today that she is my mother? With faith-filled expectancy I will await her response.

July 17

Always remember to love your neighbor; always prefer the one who tries your patience, who tests your virtue, because with her you can always merit: suffering is Love; the Law is Love.

—Traditionally attributed to St. Mariam Baouardy

W hich neighbor am I currently being called to love, and what virtue is God seeking to perfect in me through him or her?

July 18

*Prayer is sowing; contemplation the reaping of the harvest,
when the reaper is filled with wonder at the ineffable
sight of the beautiful ears of corn, which have sprung
before him from the little naked seeds that he sowed.*

—St. Isaac of Syria, "Directions on the Spiritual Life"

What are some of the "beautiful ears of corn" that I have seen sprout from past prayers? May this give me encouragement to persevere in my current petition.

July 19

*Miss no single opportunity of making some small sacrifice,
here by a smiling look, there by a kindly word; always
doing the smallest things right and doing it all for love.*

—St. Thérèse of Lisieux, *Story of a Soul*

Today I will sharpen my senses to see how many small
sacrifices I will make for love of God.

July 20

Correct one another, not in anger, but in composure, as you read in the Gospel.

—*Didache*, 15.3

What attitude of heart and demeanor mark my correction of others? What attitude of heart and demeanor mark my reception of correction?

July 21

ST. LAWRENCE OF BRINDISI (1559–1619)

Preaching of the word of God is necessary for the spiritual life, just as the planting of seed is necessary for bodily life. Preaching, therefore, is a duty that is apostolic, angelic, Christian, divine.

—From a homily of St. Lawrence of Brindisi

To whom can I preach the word today? In what way?

RECONCILIATION: A BREATH OF LIFE

I went to Confession today. And once again, I was overcome by the gracious goodness of our God. It caused me to wonder why it is that we do not use this sacrament more frequently.

It is said that St. John Paul II went to confession every day. Imagine! He, like so many others who have been raised to the altar of Christ, discovered the treasury of grace that awaits us in the sacrament even when grave sin is not present. Simply put, the Sacrament of Reconciliation is restorative. It is, after all, a sacrament of healing.

For myself this morning, I found it to be exactly that: restorative and renewing, revitalizing and redeeming. The graces received in the quiet and solitude of confronting Our Lord with our weakness and frailties, our struggles and concerns, our discouragements and frustrations are boundless.

Exposing the dark parts of our being to the rays of light that emanate from the Heart of Christ truly sets us free. The grace of this sacrament affects every part of us — our psyche, our emotions, our spiritual life, even our physiology. We are inundated with the healing love of God and, in that holy exchange of Heart-to-heart, new life comes.

What is your burden this day? Is it a deep sin for which you need to receive forgiveness? Is it a weakness from which you wish to be set free? How about discouragement, hopelessness, or despair? There is a solution. Run—don't walk—to the sacrament! Be set free!

July 22
ST. MARY MAGDALENE

*"The disciples went back home, but Mary wept
and remained standing outside the tomb." And so it
happened that the woman who stayed behind to seek
Christ was the only one to see him. For perseverance
is essential to any good deed, as the voice of truth tells
us. Whoever perseveres to the end will be saved.*

—From a homily of St. Gregory the Great

What specific lesson is God teaching me through the quote
of St. Gregory the Great?

July 23

ST. BRIDGET OF SWEDEN (1303–1373)

*O Sweet Jesus! Pierce my heart
so that my tears of penitence and love
will be my bread day and night;
May I be converted entirely to Thee,
may my heart be Thy perpetual habitation,
may my conversion be pleasing to Thee,
and may the end of my life be so praiseworthy
that I may merit Heaven and there with Thy saints,
praise Thee forever.*

—From a prayer of St. Bridget of Sweden

I will pray this prayer three times today asking the Holy Spirit to help me enter into it more deeply and fervently each time.

July 24
ST. SHARBEL OF MAKHLUF (1828–1898)

Father of truth,
Behold your Son who makes atoning
sacrifice to you.
Accept the offering:
He died for me that I might
have life.

—From a prayer of St. Sharbel

Jesus really, truly died for me! To what extent does my life reflect my gratitude?

July 25

Jesus goes before us to show us the way, both up the mountain and into heaven, and—I speak boldly—it is for us now to follow him with all speed, yearning for that heavenly vision that will give us a share in his radiance, renew our spiritual nature and transform us into his likeness, making us for ever sharers in his Godhead and raising us to heights as yet undreamed of.

—From a homily of St. Anastasius

What mountain am I ascending now? How is the glory of the Lord and heaven reflected in it? To what extent am I permitting it to renew my spiritual nature and transform me into the likeness of Jesus? What are the special graces I am receiving in it and through it?

July 26

STS. JOACHIM AND ANN, PARENTS OF THE BLESSED VIRGIN MARY

Joachim and Ann, how blessed a couple! All creation is indebted to you. For at your hands the Creator was offered a gift excelling all other gifts: a chaste mother, who alone was worthy of Him.

—From St. John Damascene's discourse on the Birth of the Virgin Mary

Just as St. Joachim and St. Ann brought the Blessed Virgin into the world through the grace of God, so too did my parents bring me into the world through the grace of God. How can I show my parents my gratitude today, whether they are living or deceased?

July 27

For we have in fact the case ... of that woman, who went to the theater and returned devil-possessed. So, when the unclean spirit was being exorcised and was pressed with the accusation that he had dared to enter a woman who believed; "and I was quite right, too," said he boldly; "for I found her on my own ground."

— Tertullian, *De Spectaculis*

To what extent do I place myself in moral jeopardy due to places I frequent, activities I engage in, and people with whom I associate?

July 28

The tree of the cross bears fruit in every season and in every land.

—Attributed to St. Thérèse Couderc

What fruit is the tree of the cross bearing in this season of my life?

July 29
ST. MARTHA

Martha and Mary were sisters, related not only by blood but also by religious aspirations. They stayed close to our Lord, and both served Him harmoniously when He was among them.

—From a homily of St. Augustine on the feast of St. Martha

How did both Martha and Mary stay close to the Lord, and how did both of them serve Him harmoniously? (See Luke 10:38–42.) In some ways, I am like both. Do I need to balance my "Martha" and my "Mary"? In what ways?

July 30
ST. PETER CHRYSOLOGUS (380–450)

There are three things through which faith stands
firm, devotion abides, and virtue endures:
prayer, fasting, and mercy. Let no one cut
these three apart—they are inseparable.

—From a homily of St. Peter Chrysologus

Which of the inseparable three have I omitted? What steps can I take to include it in my devotions so that my faith may stand firm, my devotion abide, and my virtue endure?

July 31
ST. IGNATIUS OF LOYOLA (1491–1556)

Receive, Lord, all my liberty, my memory, my understanding, and my whole will. You have given me all that I have, all I am, and I surrender it to your divine will. Give me only your love and your grace. With this I am rich enough, and I have no more to ask.

—Suscipe prayer of St. Ignatius of Loyola

Can I pray this prayer with true sincerity of heart? What may hold me back?

THE LIFE OF ST. IGNATIUS OF LOYOLA

Inigo Lopez de Loyola was born in 1491 in the Basque region of northern Spain. (He would later adopt the name Ignatius to be easier for French and Italian speakers to say.) Born into a noble house, he took an interest in military matters from a young age. Until the age of thirty, has was known as a flamboyant military man and eager dueler, attempting to live out the military legends of his people.

But in 1521, Ignatius was seriously injured by a cannonball, and during his recovery he immersed himself in spiritual reading. Shortly thereafter he hung his military equipment before an image of the Blessed Mother, foreswearing that life forever. He retreated for a time to a cave to contemplate the Lord; this is where he composed much of his most famous work, *The*

Spiritual Exercises, which remains to this day one of the most popular works of spiritual wisdom.

Ignatius spent the next nearly twenty years of his life in study at universities around Europe. This was a time of great upheaval, as the aftershocks of the Protestant Reformation were still rocking Europe. Ignatius resolved to use his learning to defend the Church against theological and philosophical attacks, and his impassioned speeches drew a group of followers to him. In 1539, he and his followers were ordained to the priesthood and formed the Society of Jesus — the Jesuits.

Ignatius's society stressed the importance of the intellectual life, missionary zeal, and absolute devotion to the Church — especially to the Holy Father. This was lived out in what became an international network of missions, schools, and universities. He was elected the first superior general of the society, in which capacity he served until his death in 1556.

Chapter Eight

Meditations

FOR

AUGUST

August 1

ST. ALPHONSUS LIGUORI, BISHOP AND
DOCTOR OF THE CHURCH (1696–1787)

*Contradictions, sickness, scruples, spiritual aridity,
and all the inner and outward torments are the chisel
with which God carves His statues for paradise.*

—Traditionally attributed to St. Alphonsus Liguori

Which chisel is God using in my life right now? How can I specifically cooperate with His sculpting that I might be fit for paradise?

August 2

FEAST OF ST. PETER JULIAN EYMARD (1811–1868)

We must keep in mind that the Holy Eucharist is Jesus Christ past, present, and future; that the Eucharist is the last development of the Incarnation and mortal life of our Savior, that in the Eucharist Jesus Christ gives us every grace; that all truths tend to an end in the Eucharist; and that there is nothing more to be added when we have said, "The Eucharist," since it is Jesus Christ.

—St. Peter Julian Eymard, *The Real Presence*

Which one description of the Eucharist given by St. Peter Julian Eymard touches me most deeply, and in what one concrete way can this enhance my gratitude of this great gift? How will I show my appreciation?

August 3

Savior, Your Crucifixion marked the end of Your mortal life; teach us to crucify ourselves and make way for our life in the Spirit. May Your Resurrection, Jesus, bring true greatness to our spiritual self, and may Your sacraments be the mirror wherein we may know that self.

—From a homily of St. Ephrem

My Lord Jesus, may this prayer of St. Ephrem resound in my heart today. Amen.

August 4
FEAST OF ST. JOHN VIANNEY, PRIEST (1786–1859)

The way to destroy bad habits is by watchfulness and by doing often those things that are opposites to one's besetting sins.

—St. John Vianney, *Thoughts of the Curé D'Ars*

What one bad habit is the Holy Spirit giving me the grace to overcome? (Which sin do I or should I confess most often?) What virtue is the opposite of it? In what three ways can I begin to exercise that virtue to help eradicate this "besetting sin"?

August 5

DEDICATION OF ST. MARY MAJOR

Who can put Mary's high honor into words? She is both mother and virgin. I am overwhelmed by the wonder of this miracle. . . . Behold then the joy of the whole universe. Let the union of God and man in the Son of the Virgin Mary fill us with awe and adoration. Let us fear and worship the undivided Trinity as we sing the praise of the ever-virgin Mary, the holy temple of God, and of God Himself, her Son and spotless Bridegroom.

—From a homily of St. Cyril of Alexandria
at the Council of Ephesus

Mary is called the "holy temple of God." How many commonalities can I think of between Mary and a temple (or church)? What does this tell me about Our Lady? What does this tell me about my parish church?

THE LIFE OF ST. JOHN VIANNEY

Jean-Baptiste-Marie Vianney, patron of parish priests, was born to devout Catholic parents in central France in 1786. Only a few years into his life, the anti-Catholic fervor of the French Revolution swept the country and the practice of the Faith was made illegal. Even so, the Vianney family traveled many miles every Sunday to attend underground Masses, and the young John was deeply impressed by the courage of the priests who continued to administer the sacraments.

Despite his interest in the priesthood, Vianney didn't begin formal studies of any kind until his father permitted him to leave the family farm at age twenty. The young man struggled in his studies, but his instructors detected a great reserve of holiness in him.

In 1809 he was drafted into the French army for Napoleon's wars of conquest, but, while praying in a village church, Vianney was left behind by his unit. An amnesty the next year allowed Vianney to continue his studies, and he was ordained in 1815.

Fr. Vianney was assigned to the tiny parish of Ars, with barely more than two hundred souls under his care. The region had been decimated, morally and economically, by the Revolution, and the people had little interest in spiritual matters. But their parish priest, or the Curé d'Ars, as he came to be known in French, set about his work faithfully.

Soon, people from the next town over, then the next region over, then from all around France, then from all around the world were coming to little Ars to experience the simple wisdom and holiness of Fr. Vianney. The centerpiece of his pastoral approach was the sacrament of Confession; he spent as many as sixteen hours per day in the confessional. St. John Vianney continued to counsel the faithful until his death in 1859.

August 6

TRANSFIGURATION OF THE LORD

*And after six days Jesus took with him Peter and James
and John, and led them up a high mountain apart by
themselves; and he was transfigured before them, and
his garments became glistening, intensely white.... And
a cloud overshadowed them, and a voice came out of
a cloud, "This is my beloved Son; listen to him."*

—Mark 9:2–3, 7

In the New Covenant, God the Father speaks to us through
His Son. What means do we have to hear His Word? Which
one do I use regularly? Which one do I need to include in my
spiritual life?

August 7

ST. CAJETAN, PRIEST (1480–1547)

My daughter, I want what is good for myself; I beg the same for you. Now there is no other way to bring this about than to ask the Virgin Mary constantly to come to you with her glorious Son. Be bold! Ask her to give you her Son, who in the Blessed Sacrament of the altar is truly the food of your soul. Readily will she give Him to you, still more readily will He come to you, giving you strength to make your way fearlessly through this dark wood. In it large numbers of our enemies lie in wait, but they cannot reach us if they see us relying on such powerful help.

—From a letter of St. Cajetan

In what one area of my life do I most need the Virgin Mary to bring her Son to me? Right this minute, with faith and confidence, I will be bold and ask Our Lady for her intercession.

August 8

ST. DOMINIC, PRIEST (1170–1221)

---

*I knew him as a steadfast follower of the apostolic
way of life. There is no doubt that he is in heaven,
sharing in the glory of the apostles themselves.*

—Pope Gregory IX on St. Dominic,
from a history of the Dominican Order

Upon my death, what would cause someone to say about
me that I was a "steadfast follower of the apostolic way
of life"? What good habit do I need to form so that this statement might one day apply to me?

August 9

ST. TERESA BENEDICTA OF THE CROSS (EDITH STEIN), MARTYR (1891–1942)

When night comes, and retrospect shows that everything was patchwork and much that one had planned left undone, when so many things rouse shame and regret, then take all as is, lay it in God's hands, and offer it up to Him. In this way we will be able to rest in Him, actually to rest and to begin the new day like a new life.

—St. Teresa Benedicta of the Cross,
"Verses for a Pentecost Novena"

Thank you, St. Teresa Benedicta of the Cross! What may I now lay in God's hands and offer up to Him, that I might "rest and begin the new day like a new life"?

August 10
ST. LAWRENCE, DEACON AND MARTYR (D. 258)

*When slow consuming had seared
The flesh of Lawrence for a space,
He calmly from his gridiron made
This terse proposal to the judge:*

*"Pray turn my body, on one side
Already broiled sufficiently,
And see how well your Vulcan's fire
Has wrought its cruel punishment."*

—Prudentius on the martyrdom of St. Lawrence

Martyrdom comes in many ways. Where am I feeling the consuming heat of martyrdom in my life right now? In what specific way can I accept this suffering with joy and strength as exemplified by St. Lawrence?

THE LIFE OF ST. TERESA BENEDICTA OF THE CROSS

St. Teresa Benedicta of the Cross was born Edith Stein in 1891 in what is now Wroclaw, in the southwest of modern Poland. Her family were observant Jews, and whereas young Edith was especially close to her mother, who insisted that her daughters be as well educated as her sons, she had become an avowed atheist by her teenage years.

Edith was a standout student of philosophy at the University of Freiburg in Germany, where she received her doctorate in 1916. She worked with some of the most notable philosophers in Europe, and was appointed as a professor at Freiburg. During this time, she lived out the topic of her philosophical work — the nature of empathy — by serving as a Red Cross nurse in war-torn southeast Europe.

In 1921 Edith read the autobiography of St. Teresa of Ávila, which brought her into the Catholic Faith. She was baptized the next year and desired to enter a convent, but her spiritual director convinced her to wait. She taught in German Catholic institutions until 1933, when Nazi racial purity laws forced her out.

No longer able to teach publicly in Germany, Edith entered a Discalced Carmelite monastery, taking the name Teresa Benedicta of the Cross. She taught nuns and wrote books, but as the Nazi threat loomed due to her Jewish heritage, her order sent her to the Netherlands. She began to prepare for internment in a concentration camp through self-denial in the monastery. Her preparations were put to use when she and other Jewish converts to the Faith were deported by the Germans after the Dutch bishops spoke out against the Nazi regime.

St. Teresa Benedicta of the Cross was killed at Auschwitz on or about August 9, 1942. She was one of the most influential Catholic thinkers of the twentieth century.

August 11
ST. CLARE, VIRGIN (1193–1253)

---

*[Jesus Christ] is the splendor of eternal glory, the brightness
of eternal light, and the mirror without cloud. Queen and
bride of Jesus Christ, look into that mirror daily and study
well your reflection, that you may adorn yourself, mind
and body, with an enveloping garment of every virtue, and
thus find yourself attired in flowers and gowns befitting
the daughter and most chaste bride of the king on high.*

—From a letter of St. Clare of Assisi

When I look into this "mirror," which virtues do I see
reflected? In what ways can I live them out today, and
in what way can I add one or two more?

August 12

If the work of God could be comprehended by reason, it would no longer be wonderful, and faith would have no merit if reason provided proof.

—From a homily of Pope St. Gregory the Great

In what one circumstance, situation, contradiction, or area of my life is God asking me to exercise faith?

August 13

STS. PONTIAN AND HIPPOLYTUS
(THIRD CENTURY)

*Do not devote your attention to the fallacies of artificial
discourses, nor the vain promises of heretics, but to
the venerable simplicity of unassuming truth.*

—St. Hippolytus, *Refutation of All Heresies*

By what I read, what I view, what I discuss, and the opinions I hold, how do I open myself up to the "fallacies of artificial discourses" prevalent in today's culture?

August 14

ST. MAXIMILIAN MARY KOLBE, MARTYR (1894–1941)

Obedience raises us beyond the limits of our littleness and puts us in harmony with God's will. Obedience is the one and the only way of wisdom and prudence for us to offer glory to God.

—From a letter of St. Maximilian Mary Kolbe

How have I experienced the truth of these words in my own life? How will this help me continue to exercise obedience?

August 15
ASSUMPTION OF THE BLESSED VIRGIN MARY

Who is she that ascends so high,
Next the Heavenly King,
Round about whom Angels fly
And her praises sing?

Who is she that, adorned with light,
Makes the sun her robe,
At whose feet the queen of night
Lays her changing globe?

To that crown direct their eyes,
Which her head attires;
There thou mayest her name descry
Writ in starry fires.

This is she in whose pure womb
Heaven's Prince remained;

Therefore in no earthly tomb
Can she be contained.

Heaven she was, which held that fire,
Whence the world took light,
And to Heaven doth now aspire
Flames with flames t' unite.

She that did so clearly shine
When our day begun,
See how bright her beams decline
Now she sits with the Sun.

—Sir John Beaumont (1583–1627)

How do you think Mary's Assumption into Heaven was anticipated by her Immaculate Conception? What hint does the poem provide?

August 16
ST. STEPHEN OF HUNGARY, KING (969–1038)

Be strong lest prosperity lift you up too much or adversity cast you down. Be humble in this life, that God may raise you up in the next. Be chaste so that you may never voluntarily bring disgrace upon anyone.

—From a letter of St. Stephen of Hungary to his son

Which piece of advice given by St. Stephen best applies to me? In what one way can I begin to practice the virtue I need?

August 17

The distance between spirituality and social action is not as great as many believe. Scripture does not reveal a spiritual man or a secular man. It speaks only of a whole man—integrated by the salvation that Christ brings.

—Ven. Fulton J. Sheen, *Those Mysterious Priests*

To what extent am I an integrated person? Do my spiritual beliefs inform my secular opinions?

DIALING HEAVEN

Some conversations etch a deep and lasting memory upon our heart. Following is one such moment from my own life that occurred on a trip to the grocery store.

"Grandma," called my almost five-year-old granddaughter from the backseat of the car.

"Yes, Julia," I replied.

"Grandma, do you know Jesus' phone number?"

"No, darling, I don't. But sometimes I sure wish I did!"

"Well, how do we talk to Him?"

"Oh," I said, "we just have to pray—even in our hearts—and He hears us."

"How do we know what He says back?"

"Julia, Jesus always answers us. But we hear His answers in our heart. We have to listen very carefully."

Things were quiet for a few minutes.

"Julia, what are you doing?" I asked.

"Shhhh, Grandma. I'm listening."

While there are times when we wish we could simply dial heaven for a quick response, we know it is in the quiet of our hearts that we most often hear the voice of God.

Are you listening today?

"And he said, 'Go forth, and stand upon the mount before the Lord.' And behold, the Lord passed by, and a great and strong wind rent the mountains, and broke in pieces the rocks before the Lord, but the Lord was not in the wind; and after the wind an earthquake, but the Lord was not in the earthquake; and after the earthquake a fire, but the Lord was not in the fire; and after the fire a still small voice" (1 Kings 19:11–12).

August 18

When one is already leading an honest and regulated life, it is far more important, in order to become a true Christian, to change the within rather than the without.

— Archbishop François Fénelon, *Christian Perfection*

According to this quote, am I ready to change the "within"? Why or why not?

August 19

ST. JOHN EUDES, PRIEST (1601–1680)

You are one with Jesus as the body is one with the head. You must, then, have one breath with Him, one soul, one life, one will, one mind, one heart. And He must be your breath, heart, love, life, your all.

—From a treatise of St. John Eudes
on the Sacred Heart of Jesus

How well does St. John Eudes's statement describe my relationship with Jesus? Where, specifically, do I need to grow?

August 20

ST. BERNARD, ABBOT AND DOCTOR OF THE CHURCH (1090–1153)

*For when God loves, all He desires is to be loved in return;
the sole purpose of His love is to be loved in the knowledge that
those who love Him are made happy by their love of Him.*

—St. Bernard, *Sermons on the Song of Songs*

According to St. Bernard, what is it that makes us happy? Conversely, what would make us unhappy? How, then, can I encourage my happiness, and what one thing can I do today to advance in this way?

August 21
ST. PIUS X (1835–1914)

*My advice is that you receive Holy Communion
frequently — if you cannot do so daily — and unite
yourself to the Savior. Make frequent visits to Him
in the solitude and silence of His tabernacle.*

—From a homily of St. Pius X to first communicants

If St. Pius X were to comment on my devotional life, to what
extent would he say I had heeded his advice?

August 22

We must forgive the society from which we come; we must forgive the ways it has hurt us. We must have forgiveness for all the pain that we have unknowingly experienced, even in the womb before our birth. We must forgive those who may not have understood us, or have seemingly neglected us, or perhaps even rejected us.

—Catherine Doherty, *Grace in Every Season*

Which aspect of forgiveness does this quote shed light upon for me in my life? How can I practically apply this wisdom?

August 23

ST. ROSE OF LIMA (1586–1617)

Let all men know that grace comes after tribulation. Let them know that the gifts of grace increase as the struggles increase. This is the only true stairway to paradise, and without the cross they can find no roads to climb to heaven.

—Our Lord to St. Rose of Lima, from a letter of the saint

What are the steps on my stairway to paradise? I will pray to the Holy Spirit and ask Him to help me identify what gifts of grace are hidden within them to help me climb the road to heaven.

THE LIFE OF ST. ROSE OF LIMA

In 1671, St. Rose of Lima became the first person born in the New World to be canonized. She was born Isabel Flores de Olivia in Peru to Spanish parents in 1586. She was given the nickname Rose as an infant when, according to a servant, her face once appeared as a rose, and she was confirmed with that name in 1597.

As a young person Rose endeavored to follow the example of St. Catherine of Siena, especially in her commitment to mortification. She fasted often and, just like Catherine, cut off her hair to avoid the attention of young men. Her parents consistently urged her to marry, and she consistently refused.

While her father absolutely prohibited her from becoming a Dominican nun, she was able (again like St. Catherine) to join the Third Order of St. Dominic. She wore the distinctive Dominican habit but lived at home, where she served the poor of the city of Lima. She would bring the sick and the hungry to her room so that she could care for them personally, and she sold handicrafts in order to help support her family and in order to have more to give to the poor.

From the time she joined the Dominicans at age twenty until her death eleven years later, it is said that she refused to sleep more than two hours per night so that she could spend more time in prayer. When she died in 1617, all the public officials of Lima came to the city's cathedral for her funeral.

August 24

ST. BARTHOLOMEW, APOSTLE

The Apostles were the nucleus of the Church, the new Israel, the first visible manifestation of Christ's Mystical Body.

—Ven. Fulton J. Sheen, *The World's First Love*

In what one way can I follow the apostles today and be a "visible manifestation of Christ's Mystical Body?"

August 25

ST. JOSEPH CALASANZ, PRIEST (1557–1648)

Like the twigs of plants the young are easily influenced,
as long as someone works to change their souls.

—From the writings of St. Joseph Calasanz

What young person am I called to influence, and how can I work to nurture his or her soul today?

August 26

Nothing half-hearted for me — I will follow
Christ with all my heart and soul.

—St. Thérèse of Lisieux, *Story of a Soul* (paraphrase)

Can I make this same claim? Where might I prove to be half-hearted in following Christ?

August 27

ST. MONICA (331–387)

---

*One thing only I ask you, that you remember me
at the altar of the Lord wherever you may be.*

—St. Monica, reported by her son,
St. Augustine, in his *Confessions*

What holy soul may benefit by my remembrance at the altar? I promise to do so for the next month.

August 28

ST. AUGUSTINE, BISHOP AND DOCTOR OF THE CHURCH (354–430)

You have created us for Yourself, and our hearts are restless till they rest in You.

—St. Augustine, *Confessions*

In what areas am I restless? In what specific ways can I bring God into this area of my life?

August 29

MARTYRDOM OF ST. JOHN THE BAPTIST

His persecutors had demanded not that he should deny Christ, but only that he should keep silent about the truth. But to endure temporal agonies for the sake of the truth was not a heavy burden for such men as John; rather it was easily borne and even desirable, for he knew eternal joy would be his reward.

—from a homily of St. Bede the Venerable

What am I willing to endure for the sake of the truth—about abortion, euthanasia, stem-cell research, same-sex unions? How can I best proclaim the truth about these given my state of life and my personal circumstances?

August 30

When a person loves another dearly, he desires strongly to be close to the other: therefore, why be afraid to die? Death brings us to God!

— Traditionally attributed to St. Josephine Bakhita

What is my honest attitude toward death? According to St. Josephine, what does the barometer indicate about my love of God? What can I do to encourage my love of Him?

August 31

One must see God in everyone.

—Traditionally attributed to St. Catherine Labouré

It is often easy to see God in people we love or admire, but quite difficult to see Him in those we dislike or disdain. Today, I will look to see God in the person who is presently causing me the most heartache and pain.

Chapter Nine

Meditations

FOR

SEPTEMBER

September 1

Isn't it absurd to send children out to jobs and to school, and to do all you can to prepare them for these, and yet not to "bring them up in the discipline and instruction of the Lord" (Eph. 6:4)? . . . Discipline is needed, not eloquence; character, not cleverness; deeds, not words. These gain a man the kingdom.

—From a homily of St. John Chrysostom

On my "wish list" for me and for my children, how near to the top is salvation? What am I doing to make it number one, and in what specific ways am I following through to attain that goal?

September 2

So you have failed? . . . You have not failed;
you have gained experience. Forward!

—St. Josemaría Escrivá, *The Way*

How does St. Josemaría's quote help me think about my most recent failure? What about the one that has bothered me for years? What experience have I gained, and how does that help me to move forward now?

September 3

ST. GREGORY THE GREAT, POPE AND DOCTOR OF THE CHURCH (540–604)

Many people are pleased by what they hear, and sincerely resolve to pursue the good. Yet when adversity and suffering come, they soon abandon their good works.

—From a homily of St. Gregory the Great

In what area is my resolve weakening today? With that in mind I pray:

Heavenly Father, today I ask you to give me the grace to "hang on and hang in" regarding (mention a situation or area in your life). Give me the strength, fortitude, patience, and perseverance I need. In Jesus' name I pray. Amen.

St. Gregory the Great, pray for me.

THE LIFE OF ST. GREGORY
THE GREAT

Gregory was born around the year 540 into one of the most prominent families in Rome. His father had been a senator and prefect of Rome, the highest civil position in the city; Gregory later filled this role as well. His mother, Silvia, and two aunts on his father's side have been canonized.

Despite his wealth and status, Gregory was drawn to the monastic life that had been popularized earlier in the fifth century by St. Benedict. He renovated his family's enormous Roman villa into a monastery and then lived there as a monk for several years until being called to a diplomatic post by Pope Pelagius II.

Gregory became the first monk to become pope in 590 when he was promptly selected by the Roman clergy and faithful. He wrote to many that he did not desire the papacy and that he would have preferred to remain a contemplative monk. But he made the most of his pontificate.

Among Pope Gregory's accomplishments, in no particular order, are: enduring liturgical and musical reforms, permanent establishment of papal supremacy over far-flung bishops, enforcement of Church discipline regarding priestly celibacy, and sending St. Augustine of Canterbury to evangelize the pagans of the British Isles. We can thank Pope Gregory for the fact that the Church in Rome became the center of medieval European life.

All the while, Pope Gregory established a sophisticated system to deliver assistance to the needy of Rome; he considered the wealth of the Church to be the property of the poor. He also created a new papal title that is used to this day: Servant of the Servants of God.

Pope St. Gregory the Great died on March 12, 604. It is said that he was immediately canonized by the acclamation of the people.

September 4

The Magdalene, most of all, is the model I like to follow. That boldness of hers, which would be so amazing if it weren't the boldness of a lover, won the heart of Jesus.

—St. Thérèse of Lisieux, *Story of a Soul* (paraphrase)

In what specific way can I, like Mary Magdalene, boldly show my love for Jesus today? When I do, I will thank "the Magdalene" for her good example.

September 5

Ceremonies may be shadows, but they are the shadows of great truths, and it is essential that they should be carried out with the greatest possible attention.

—Traditionally attributed to St. Vincent de Paul

Where do I most need to improve my attention during the Holy Sacrifice of the Mass? What positive step to doing so can I take today?

September 6

If any bad thought comes to you, make the Sign of the Cross, or say the Our Father, or strike your breast, and try to think of something else. If you do that, the thought will actually be winning you merit, because you will be resisting it.

—From a letter of St. Teresa of Ávila

What a transforming way to look at temptation! Today I will follow St. Teresa's advice and examine my conscience at day's end to see how well I have done.

September 7

Mount Calvary is the academy of love.

—St. Francis de Sales, *Treatise on the Love of God*

Contemplating the scene of the Crucifixion, what three persons do I see enrolled in this "academy of love" besides Jesus, and how is their love expressed? Today, in what ways can I follow their example, and in what ways am I willing to enroll in the academy?

September 8
NATIVITY OF THE BLESSED VIRGIN MARY

Dipped in the instincts of heaven,
Robed in the garments of earth,
Maiden and Mother and Queen,
Wearing each crown at thy birth:

Threefold thy gift to the world,
Pluck'd from God's ripening sky,
Tending the altar of life,
Kindred to angels on high.

— "Woman," Thomas O'Hagan

Tending the altar of life …" In addition to bringing Jesus into the world, how else does Sacred Scripture show Mary as "mother"? I will do likewise in three ways today as a special birthday present to her.

September 9

ST. PETER CLAVER, PRIEST (1581–1654)

To love God as He ought to be loved, we must be detached from all temporal love. We must love nothing but Him, or if we love anything else, we must love it only for His sake.

—Traditionally attributed to St. Peter Claver

What one "temporal love" am I most attached to? How can I cultivate a spirit of detachment in relation to it?

September 10

The saints were so completely dead to themselves that they cared very little whether others agreed with them or not.

—St. John Vianney, "On Pride"

According to St. John Vianney's quote, how much have I died to myself? (How important is it to me to win an argument? Make my point? Have the last word? Speak the truth when inconvenient? Defend the truth in the face of ridicule?)

September 11

For in this way especially does a friend differ from a flatterer: the flatterer speaks to give pleasure, but the friend refrains from nothing, even that which causes pain.

—From a letter of St. Basil the Great

A true friend speaks—and hears—the truth in love. Am I a true friend, both in speaking the truth and in receiving the truth? Why or why not?

September 12

I have never succeeded when I have spoken with the faintest suspicion of hardness. One must be ever on one's guard not to embitter the heart, if one wishes to move the mind.

—Traditionally attributed to St. Vincent de Paul

According to St. Vincent de Paul, how successful am I in speaking the truth to others? Does my own experience bear out his advice? How can I best prepare myself to speak the truth in love and to receive the truth in love?

September 13

ST. JOHN CHRYSOSTOM, BISHOP AND DOCTOR OF THE CHURCH (349–407)

Though the waves of the sea and the anger of princes are roused against me, they are less to me than a spider's web . . . not what this fellow or that would have me do, but what [God] wants me to do. . . . If God wants something, let it be done!

—From a homily of St. John Chrysostom

To what extent am I more influenced by the desires of others than by God's desires? I will examine my decisions based on this for the next week.

IT'S HABIT FORMING

Yesterday morning while I was making my bed, a question entered my mind: "Why is it that it's so easy to develop a bad habit and so difficult to acquire a good one?" The answer came as I tucked the sheet and fluffed my pillow.

A bad habit rises out of our passions—usually our disordered passions. Even if there's nothing wrong with a desire itself, say, for good food or clothing, lack of self-discipline can make it a vice, such as overeating or overspending. This is rooted in our natural inclination to sin.

A good habit, on the other hand, requires order, constraint, and self-mastery. It requires taming unbridled desires through sacrifice. Doing this goes against the grain of our fallen nature, and so it doesn't bring us pleasure—at least initially. What, then, do we do? In addition to praying for all of the supernatural help and grace we need and making good use of the sacraments, we employ our will and begin to reorder ourselves toward the good, the holy, and the truly beautiful.

As we do so, we begin to seek a different kind of pleasure—one rooted in the things of God rather than the things of the world. One that seeks the eternal rather than the temporal. One that leads us to truth rather than illusion.

Doing so yields not only good habits and their accompanying virtues, but that which good habits and their virtues bring—true and abiding happiness.

September 14
EXALTATION OF THE HOLY CROSS

Faithful Cross, above all other, one and only noble tree.... Sweet the wood, and sweet the iron, and thy load, most sweet is He.

— Venantius Fortunatus, *Crux Fidelis*

In what one area of my life have I most recently seen the liberating power of Christ's Cross? Today, I will offer a sacrifice of praise for His gracious mercy.

September 15

OUR LADY OF SORROWS

They warned Our Lady for the Child
That was Our Blessed Lord,
And She took Him into the desert wild,
Over the camel's ford.

And a long song She sang to Him
And a short story told:
And She wrapped Him in a woolen cloak
To keep Him from the cold.

But when Our Lord was grown a man
The Rich they dragged Him down,
And they crucified Him in Golgotha,
Out and beyond the Town.

They crucified Him on Calvary,
Upon an April day;
And because He had been her little Son
She followed Him all the way.

Our Lady stood beside the Cross,
A little space apart,
And when She heard Our Lord cry out
A sword went through Her Heart.

They laid Our Lord in a marble tomb,
Dead, in a winding sheet.
But Our Lady stands above the world
With the white Moon at Her feet.

—"Our Lord and Our Lady," Hilaire Belloc

Of the seven swords that pierced Our Lady's heart, how many are represented in this poem? How do her swords relate to the pains of my heart?

September 16

STS. CORNELIUS, POPE, AND CYPRIAN, BISHOP, MARTYRS (210–258)

Petition is ineffectual when it is a barren entreaty that implores God. . . . The Holy Scripture instructs us saying, "Prayer is good with fasting and almsgiving."

—St. Cyprian, "On the Lord's Prayer"

What is my most pressing petition to God? What can I do to make it more effective? Am I willing? Why or why not?

September 17

ST. ROBERT BELLARMINE, BISHOP AND DOCTOR OF THE CHURCH (1542–1621)

Prosperity and adversity, wealth and poverty, health and sickness, honors and humiliations, life and death, in the mind of the wise man, are not sought for their own sake, nor avoided for their own sake. But if they contribute to the glory of God and your eternal happiness, then they are good and should be sought. If they detract from this, they are evil and must be avoided.

—St. Robert Bellarmine, *On the Ascent to the Mind of God*

What current joy and what current sorrow has God permitted me to contribute to my good?

September 18

---

*We would all much better mend our ways if we
were as ready to pray for one another as we are
to offer one another reproach and rebuke.*

—From the writings of St. Thomas More (paraphrase)

What step does St. Thomas More offer that will help me in my dealings with others—especially when a difficult conversation is at hand? How will his advice affect me and the other party?

September 19

The Christian prays in every situation, in his walks for recreation, in his dealing with others, in silence, in reading, in all rational pursuits.

—St. Clement of Alexandria

According to St. Clement, would I be called a Christian? How can I implement his advice in practical ways beginning today?

September 20

ST. ANDREW KIM TAEGON, PRIEST AND MARTYR, AND ST. PAUL CHONG HASANG AND COMPANIONS, MARTYRS (NINETEENTH CENTURY)

Hold fast to the will of God and with all your heart fight the good fight under the leadership of Jesus; conquer again the diabolical power of this world that Christ has already vanquished.

—From the final words of St. Andrew Kim Taegon

Given the tenor of our times, in what ways am I called by God to "hold fast" and conquer the diabolical powers of the world? In what areas of influence can I be effective in some way?

September 21

ST. MATTHEW, APOSTLE AND EVANGELIST

*The other Evangelists, out of respect for Matthew, did
not call him by his common name, so they said Levi.
But Matthew called himself Matthew and a publican
[tax collector], that he might show his readers that no
one ought to despair of salvation . . . since he himself
suddenly changed from a publican to an apostle.*

—from St. Jerome's Commentary
on the Gospel of Matthew

What sudden change might God be asking me to make
today? St. Matthew, pray for me.

September 22

---

*You persist in being worldly, superficial,
scatterbrained, because you are a coward. What is
it but cowardice not to want to face yourself?*

—St. Josemaría Escrivá, *The Way*

Ouch! What am I too cowardly to admit about myself?
What remedy can I employ to move from "coward" to
"conqueror" in this area?

September 23

ST. PIO OF PIETRELCINA, PRIEST (1887–1968)

When a soul does everything possible and trusts divine mercy, why would Jesus reject such a spirit? If you have given and consecrated everything to God, why be afraid?

—From the writings of St. Padre Pio

The evil one seeks to discourage us through fear. But, as St. Pio reminds us, God calls us to trust. What one fear is the evil one sowing in my heart to discourage me? What does St. Pio recommend that I do? I will do it now and ask the intercession of St. Pio.

September 24

Our self-will is so subtle, so deeply rooted within us, so covered with excuses and defended by false reasoning, that it seems to be a demon. When we cannot do our own will in one way, we do it in another, under all kinds of pretexts.

—St. Catherine of Genoa, *Life and Teachings*

What might I currently be covering with excuses, false reasoning, or pretexts so that I might have my way?

THE LIFE OF ST. PADRE PIO

K nown affectionately around the world as Padre Pio (Father
Pius), St. Pio was born Francesco Forgione in southern
Italy in 1887. His parents were simple farmers who loved the
Church; Padre Pio reported later in life that at the age of five
he resolved to dedicate his life to the Lord. As a teenager he
entered the novitiate with the Capuchin friars.

Francesco had always been a sickly child, and his health
problems persisted as Friar Pio. He was even permitted to live
at home for several years while maintaining his status with the
Capuchins. After a brief compulsory military service during
World War I, he settled into community life in 1918. That
year he would manifest the signs that would make him famous
around the world.

As early as 1911, Padre Pio experienced symptoms of stigmata. But in 1918, after undergoing a month-long trial of intense spiritual and physical pain, he received the five wounds of Christ permanently. He was embarrassed by the public nature of his trials (he would have preferred the pain without the wounds), and so he always covered his hands and feet.

Church officials were initially skeptical of Padre Pio's experiences. He was for a time forbidden from hearing confessions or saying Mass publicly. But new information and public acclaim for the priest's spiritual gifts slowly softened the Vatican's approach. By the 1940s, Pope Pius XII was actively encouraging pilgrims to visit the stigmatist.

But Padre Pio's fame was not just related to his mystical experiences. Pilgrims flocked to him for his simple but profound spiritual wisdom. He exhorted all Catholics to receive the sacraments regularly and to perform regular meditations and examinations of conscience.

About fifty years after first receiving the stigmata, Padre Pio died in 1968.

September 25

*In the same way that a powerful medicine cures
an illness, so illness itself is a medicine to cure a
passion. And there is much profit of soul in bearing
illness quietly and giving thanks to God.*

—Amma Syncletica, reported
in *The Sayings of the Fathers*

Sometimes God permits an illness or contradiction in our life so that we might grow in virtue, be healed, or attain a deeper spiritual commitment. Could this be the case for me in a current difficulty? "We know that in everything God works for good with those who love him, who are called according to his purpose" (Romans 8:28).

September 26

He causes his prayers to be of more avail to himself, who offers them also for others.

—Pope St. Gregory the Great, *Morals*

How does praying for another help me as well as the other person?

September 27

ST. VINCENT DE PAUL, PRIEST (1581–1660)

When we are discussing things which it is good and proper to talk about, we should hold back any details which would not be for God's glory, or which could harm some other person, or which would make us foolishly smug. In actual practice this virtue is about choosing the right way to do things.

—From a rule of St. Vincent de Paul

Calumny, detraction, and slander: these are three ways I can sin against my neighbor with my words. Taking an honest look, have I been guilty of any of these in the last twenty-four hours? In the last week? In the last month? I will confess this sin and actively pursue ways to tame my tongue.

September 28

ST. WENCESLAUS, MARTYR (907–935)

Brother, what are you trying to do!

—St. Wenceslaus to Boleslaus, his brother,
who conspired to assassinate him

Even at the moment his brother tried to murder him, Wenceslaus responded with loving concern for him and his salvation. Is there a loved one from whom I am estranged or with whom there has been a rift? How is God asking me to be a peacemaker and healer of the breach? St. Wenceslaus, pray for me.

September 29

ARCHANGELS MICHAEL, GABRIEL, AND RAPHAEL

The angels have five duties. The first is to continually sing hymns and praises to their Creator. The second duty is to present the prayers of mortals to God and commend them with their petitions. The third duty consists in their being sent as messengers to declare what God wants to declare. The fourth duty is protecting men, whether as individuals or groups. The last duty is to serve as soldiers and armed leaders. Let good men love their fellow citizens, the angels.

—St. Robert Bellarmine, *Spiritual Writings*

One way I can show the angels my love is by imitating them in their duties. In what ways can I do this?

September 30

ST. JEROME, PRIEST AND DOCTOR OF THE CHURCH (340–420)

For if, as Paul says, Christ is the power of God and the wisdom of God, and if the man who does not know Scripture does not know the power and wisdom of God, then ignorance of Scripture is ignorance of Christ.

—St. Jerome, *Commentary on Isaiah*

How well do I know Christ? What can I do to know Him better?

Chapter Ten

Meditations

FOR

OCTOBER

October 1

FEAST OF ST. THÉRÈSE OF THE CHILD JESUS, VIRGIN AND DOCTOR OF THE CHURCH (1873–1897)

I am only a very little soul, who can only offer very little things to our Lord.

—St. Thérèse of Lisieux, *Story of a Soul*

Today, in honor of St. Thérèse's feast day, I will find three "very little things" that I can offer to our Lord. May they help me grow in virtue.

THE LIFE OF ST. THÉRÈSE
OF LISIEUX

Known as St. Thérèse of the Child Jesus and as the Little Flower, Thérèse Martin was born on January 2, 1873, in northeast France. Her mother, Marie-Azélie (known as Zélie), and her father, Louis, had both desired to enter religious life, but neither were able to do so. Their desires were fulfilled in their four daughters, all of whom became nuns. In 2015, Zélie and Louis became the first married couple to be canonized.

Thérèse's carefree childhood was cut short at the age of four when her mother died from breast cancer. The family moved north to Lisieux, and although they lived reasonably comfortably, young Thérèse was a melancholy child. The dark period of her childhood ended suddenly at Christmas, 1886, when she felt the peace of the Child Jesus wash over her.

She resolved then to enter the local Carmelite convent, but at fourteen she was too young. The next year, her family was able to meet with Pope Leo XIII. She fell at his feet and begged him to permit her to enter the Carmel. He gently told her to be obedient to the prioress. Later that year, Thérèse was permitted to enter the Carmel in Lisieux.

Thérèse didn't always have an easy time in the monastery. She hated being away from her family, and she struggled to follow the rules. She found peace in what came to be known her "little way" of holiness: entrusting her little daily faults to God's mercy while performing little acts of love for God and neighbor.

St. Thérèse of Lisieux contracted tuberculosis at the age of twenty-three. She found sweetness in her suffering, which astounded even her doctors. She died a year later and within thirty years was canonized by Pope Pius XI.

October 2

GUARDIAN ANGELS

They come, God's messengers of love,
They come from realms of peace above,
From homes of never-fading light,
From blissful mansions ever bright.

They come to watch around us here,
To soothe our sorrow, calm our fear:
Ye heavenly guides, speed not away,
God willeth you with us to stay.

But chiefly at its journey's end
'Tis yours the spirit to befriend,
And whisper to the willing heart,
'O Christian soul, in peace depart.'

To us the zeal of angels give,
With love to serve thee while we live;
To us an angel-guard supply,

When on the bed of death we lie.

To God the Father, God the Son,
And God the Spirit, Three in One,
From all above and all below
Let joyful praise unceasing flow.

—Robert Campbell

Today, I will make a fifteen-minute meditation recalling the many ways my guardian angel has protected me spiritually and physically through the years. Thank you, guardian angel, for all you have done for me.

October 3

We should not wish for anything but what
comes to us from moment to moment,
exercising ourselves nonetheless for good.

—St. Catherine of Genoa, reported in *The Mystical*
Element of Religion, Volume 1, by Friedrich von Hügel

Do I live in the grace of the present moment, or am I busy bemoaning the past or worrying about the future? How is this present moment calling forth from me the opportunity to exercise grace for the good?

October 4

ST. FRANCIS OF ASSISI (1182–1226)

Men lose all the material things they leave behind them in this world, but they carry with them the reward of their charity and the alms they give. For these they will receive from the Lord the reward and recompense they deserve.

—From a letter of St. Francis of Assisi

When I stand before the Lord, how full of charitable works and gifts to the poor will my hands be? What one act of charity can I perform today to show my love of God and neighbor?

October 5

Christ made my soul beautiful with the jewels of grace and virtue. I belong to Him whom the angels serve.

—Traditionally attributed to St. Agnes

What "jewels of grace and virtue" do I possess? I will praise and thank God for them and seek to live them to the full.

October 6

ST. BRUNO (1035–1101)

When you observe true obedience with prudence and enthusiasm, it is clear that you wisely pick the most delightful and nourishing fruit of divine Scripture.

—From a letter of St. Bruno to his fellow Carthusians

Why does St. Bruno consider obedience to be the most delightful and nourishing fruit of divine Scripture? In what one way can I practice obedience with prudence and enthusiasm today?

October 7

OUR LADY OF THE ROSARY

Say the Rosary every day. . . . Pray, pray a lot and offer sacrifices for sinners. . . . I am Our Lady of the Rosary. Only I will be able to help you. . . . In the end my Immaculate Heart will triumph.

—*Our Lady of Fátima*

To what extent am I personally heeding Our Blessed Mother's plea? In what one way can I be more diligent?

October 8

We need heralds of the Gospel who are experts in humanity, who know in depth the hearts of the men of today, who participate in their joys and hopes, concerns and sorrows, and at the same time are persons in love with God.

—From an address of St. John Paul II

Given my state in life, in what three ways can I be a herald of the gospel? And, given my state in life, how can I be a contemplative?

October 9

ST. DENIS, BISHOP AND MARTYR, AND COMPANION MARTYRS (THIRD CENTURY)

Today it is fashionable to talk about the poor.
Unfortunately it is not fashionable to talk with them.

—St. Teresa of Calcutta, reported by John Scally
in *Mother Teresa: The Irish Connection*

Who are the poor in my midst? How can I reach out to them, person to person?

October 10

---

*There is no sin nor wrong that gives a man such a
foretaste of hell in this life as anger and impatience.*

—From a letter of St. Catherine of Siena

What is it about anger and impatience that creates a hellish
sensation? In what one way can I cooperate with grace
today to channel anger's energy in a positive direction?

October 11

Death must be active within us if life
also is to be active within us.

—St. Ambrose, *Death as a Blessing*

Reflect on the wisdom of these words. What interior death am I experiencing now? What new life am I seeing in its place?

October 12

You will accomplish more by kind words and a courteous manner than by anger or sharp rebuke, which should never be used except in necessity.

—Traditionally attributed to St. Angela Merici

Which one virtue do I most need to acquire to follow St. Angela's advice when I am in the midst of a difficult exchange with another?

GOD AND DINOSAURS

Gabriel, age eight, came home from school with a freshly completed art project—a paper dinosaur. It was painted bright green and had a toilet-paper tube for a skeleton. Gabriel loved his dinosaur.

He carried his dinosaur with him everywhere. He placed it on the floor next to him when he was playing. He set it on the table when he was eating. He even perched it on the back of the couch while he watched his favorite show. And he treated it to a trip to the restaurant when the family went out to dinner.

Gabriel's father asked him what it was that so attracted him to his dinosaur. Gabriel simply responded, "I made it."

Gabriel's answer brought a smile to my face and joy to my heart. And it made me think of God.

Like Gabriel's attention to his dinosaur, God's eyes are always upon us. We are never out of His sight. We are the "apple of his eye," the center of His vision.

If we asked our Heavenly Father why he keeps us in His gaze, His answer would be the same as Gabriel's: "I made you."

"I have loved you with an everlasting love; therefore I have continued my faithfulness to you" (Jeremiah 31:3).

October 13

If I had to advise parents, I should tell them to take great care about the people with whom their children associate.... Much harm may result from bad company, and we are inclined by nature to follow what is worse rather than what is better.

—St. Teresa of Ávila, her *Life*

How have I seen this truth play out in my life? Are there people with whom my children are associating who could influence them in the wrong direction? Is there a practical and loving step I can take today to resolve this situation?

October 14

ST. CALLISTUS I, POPE
AND MARTYR (D. 222)

*In time of persecution the battle wins the crown, but
in peace it is the testimony of a good conscience.*

—from a treatise of St. Cyprian

This quote applies well to St. Callistus who won the crown of martyrdom strengthened by a good conscience that was formed according to the will of God. In what three ways would my conscience testify *for* me in such a situation, and in what three ways would it testify *against* me?

October 15

ST. TERESA OF ÁVILA, VIRGIN AND DOCTOR OF THE CHURCH (1515–1582)

Whenever we think of Christ we should recall the love that led him to bestow on us so many graces and favors, and also the great love God showed in giving us in Christ a pledge of his love; for love calls for love in return. Let us strive to keep this always before our eyes and to rouse ourselves to love him.

—St. Teresa of Ávila, "Let Us Always Be Mindful of Christ's Love"

Three ways we can rouse ourselves to love Jesus more are: (1) to be consistent with our daily prayer; (2) to make use of the sacraments more regularly; and (3) to perform loving acts toward others to manifest our love for Him. Which of these three do I need to implement in my spiritual life?

October 16

ST. MARGARET MARY ALACOQUE, VIRGIN (1647–1690)

It seems to me that our Lord's earnest desire to have His Sacred Heart honored in a special way is directed toward renewing the effects of redemption in our souls. For the Sacred Heart is an inexhaustible fountain and its sole desire is to pour itself out into the hearts of the humble so as to free them and prepare them to lead lives according to his good pleasure.

—From a letter of St. Margaret Mary Alacoque

In what one way can I honor the Sacred Heart of Jesus more?

THE LIFE OF ST. MARGARET MARY ALACOQUE

Margaret Alacoque was born in Burgundy (now southeast France) in 1647. In her preteen years she suffered a years-long illness that kept her confined to bed. At the age of thirteen she promised the Blessed Mother that, should she be healed, she would enter religious life. It is said that at that moment she was cured. In thanksgiving, she added "Mary" to her name.

At the age of seventeen, Margaret Mary's mother insisted that she pursue marriage. The family's fortune had just been restored after legal troubles following the death of Margaret Mary's father, and so the young woman reasoned that the change in circumstances voided her childhood vow.

But after an evening at Carnival, she had a vision of Christ's Passion. Her bloody Savior scolded her for abandoning her vow but also showed her the love He had in His Heart for her for having made the vow to begin with. After this vision, Margaret Mary entered the Visitation Convent.

Now, Margaret had been receiving visions of Jesus since childhood. In fact, she thought it was a perfectly normal experience. But in the convent, those visions intensified, and the Lord revealed to her the devotion to His Sacred Heart. The devotion consisted of reception of the Eucharist on the first Friday of the month preceded on Thursday by a Holy Hour of adoration and meditation on Jesus' agony in the garden.

Margaret Mary's fellow sisters, along with other Church officials, were doubtful of her innovative visions. But the nun persisted in her devotion, in charity and obedience, and soon the sisters were won over. St. Margaret Mary Alacoque died on October 17, 1690; the devotion to the Sacred Heart of Jesus was officially approved by the Church seventy-five years later.

October 17

ST. IGNATIUS OF ANTIOCH, BISHOP AND MARTYR (D. 107)

No earthly pleasures, no kingdoms of this world can benefit me in any way. I prefer death in Christ Jesus to power over the furthest limits of the earth. He who died in place of us is the one object of my quest.

—From a letter of St. Ignatius of Antioch

Dear Lord, St. Ignatius of Antioch was ready to be torn apart by a lion rather than to be separated from you. In light of his zeal, my own fervor is so weak. Give me courage and strength to proclaim your Truth no matter the cost. Heal me in those areas where I am weak. Fill me with your divine love. And renew me in faith and hope. I pray this in the name of Jesus my Lord. Amen. St. Ignatius, pray for me.

October 18

ST. LUKE, EVANGELIST

Behold, I am the handmaid of the Lord; let it be to me according to your word.

—Luke 1:38

Dear Lord, You inspired St. Luke through the power of the Holy Spirit to comprehend the great mysteries of Your life, death, and Resurrection. Draw me more deeply into these mysteries. Give me light to see truth, wisdom to follow truth, and faith to apply truth. I pray this in the name of Jesus Christ, Who is the Truth. Amen.

St. Luke, pray for me.

October 19

ST. ISAAC JOGUES AND JEAN DE BRÉBEUF, PRIESTS AND MARTYRS, AND THEIR COMPANIONS, MARTYRS (D. 1648)

For two days now I have experienced a great desire to be a martyr and to endure all the torments the martyrs suffered.

—from the journal of St. Jean De Brébeuf

Take delight in the Lord, and he will give you the desires of your heart" (Psalm 37:4). How do this passage and the above quotation help me to have confidence in what God's will may be for me?

October 20

ST. PAUL OF THE CROSS, PRIEST (1694–1775)

It is very good and holy to consider the passion of our Lord and to meditate on it, for by this sacred path we reach union with God.

—From a letter of St. Paul of the Cross

As I consider the passion of Our Lord, what one aspect of it speaks most deeply to my heart? Today, I will meditate on it. What is the Lord saying to me through it? What is my response back to Him?

THE LIFE OF ST. PAUL
OF THE CROSS

The founder of the Passionists was born Paolo Francesco Danei in northern Italy in 1694. His family was strong in the Faith, and he led a quiet childhood. It is said that at the age of nineteen Paul was profoundly affected by the *Treatise on the Love of God* by St. Francis de Sales, and he committed himself to a life of prayer.

After a brief interlude assisting his father to fight the Turks who were threatening Venice, Paul helped out with the family store. He rebuffed suggestions of marriage and soon found himself drawn not just to enter the priesthood but to form a new religious community.

In prayer, Paul had discerned that contemplation of the Lord's Passion was essential to holiness. His community would be dedicated to such contemplation, clothed in a black tunic with a simple emblem: a cross over a heart with the words "Passion of Jesus Christ" within it.

The first person to join Paul in forming this community was his brother, John Baptist. They were ordained to the priesthood together in 1727, and they set about preaching and ministering to the people, spreading devotion to the Passion. The first Passionist house, or "retreat," was opened ten years later with nine members.

The first Passionist communities were austere, befitting the subject of contemplation to which they were devoted. Members would celebrate the divine office together and spend at least three hours in personal contemplative prayer every day. By the time of St. Paul of the Cross's death in 1775, there were 180 Passionists in 12 retreats around Rome. The congregation now has houses around the world.

October 21

ST. MARGUERITE D'YOUVILLE

*All the wealth in the world cannot be compared with
the happiness of living together happily united.*

—Traditionally attributed to St. Margaret of Youville

How many waking hours a week does my family spend together in a common activity? Is there something in my life or in the life of my family that is compromising our "living together happily united"? What resolution am I willing to make?

October 22

As you work, as you come and go, as you pass among the crowds, to be a contemplative will mean simply that you try to turn to Jesus within you and enter into conversation with Him, as with the one you love most in the world.

—Little Sister Magdeleine of Jesus, *The Green Booklet*

Today, I will practice my call to be a contemplative in the world, making use of every opportunity the Lord gives me to enter into conversation with Him in the inner confines of my heart. This evening, I will cast a retrospective glance over the course of the day to see the results of my effort.

October 23

ST. JOHN OF CAPISTRANO, PRIEST (1386–1456)

Those who are called to the table of the Lord must glow with the brightness that comes from the good example of a praiseworthy and blameless life.

—St. John of Capistrano, "Mirror of the Clergy"

Who are the holy priests who have ministered to me in my life? In what one way have they or did they glow with the brightness of a praiseworthy life? I will pray for them and in gratitude to God for their vocation.

October 24

Novelists are generally great liars.

—St. Jean-Baptiste de la Salle, *On the Duty of a Christian Toward God*

Are there any dangerous spiritual novelties, such as New Age spirituality, that I have dallied with or to which I have become attached? What is this quote telling me, and what do I need to do?

October 25

Let us open our hearts to admit all humanity. At the touch of the divine let us resound with every gracious thought, every human affection; let us learn to find in each soul the point at which it is still in touch with the Infinite God.

—Servant of God Elisabeth Leseur,
The Secret Diary of Elisabeth Leseur

Today, I am going to look at that one person who is most difficult in my life and seek to find that point in his or her soul that is still in touch with the Infinite God. To do so, I will pray to see three virtues that he or she exemplifies.

October 26

Woman's soul is . . . fashioned to be a shelter in which other souls may unfold. Both spiritual companionship and spiritual motherliness are not limited to the physical spouse and mother relationships, but they extend to all people with whom woman comes into contact.

—St. Teresa Benedicta of the Cross (Edith Stein), "Fundamental Principles of Women's Education"

How has my soul been a shelter in which other souls may unfold? In what one way can I practice spiritual motherliness today?

October 27

*We are pilgrims and strangers on earth. Pilgrims sleep
in tents and sometimes cross deserts, but the thought of
their homeland makes them forget everything else.*

—From the writings of Bl. Charles de Foucauld

To what extent does my thought of heaven help to make my struggles in life more bearable?

October 28

FEAST OF ST. SIMON AND ST. JUDE, APOSTLES

You did not choose me, but I chose you and appointed you that you should go and bear fruit and that your fruit should abide.

—John 15:16

This passage from Scripture applies to me just as certainly as it applied to the apostles. In what specific ways am I bearing fruit that will last? How can I plant one more seed today?

October 29

What a weakness it is to love Jesus Christ only when He caresses us, and to be cold immediately when He afflicts us. This is not true love. Those who love thus, love themselves too much to love God with all their heart.

—St. Margaret Mary Alacoque, reported
in a biography by Fr. Albert Barry

Ponder this quotation in light of St. John Paul II's definition of love as an act of total self-donation. Am I truly willing to love God and others in this way?

October 30

*Human government is derived from the divine
government and should imitate it.*

—St. Thomas Aquinas, *Summa Theologica*, II-II, Q. 10, art. 11

Consider this quotation in light of our right to vote and any upcoming elections. How would a well-formed conscience direct me to vote?

October 31

It is a mark of the evil spirit to take on the appearance of an angel of light. He begins by whispering thoughts that are suited to a devout soul, and ends by suggesting his own.

—St. Ignatius of Loyola, *Spiritual Exercises*

What should be the standards against which I evaluate my thoughts and ideas?

Chapter Eleven

Meditations

FOR

NOVEMBER

November 1

ALL SAINTS

The saints have no need of honor from us; neither does our devotion add the slightest thing to what is theirs. But I tell you, when I think of them, I feel myself enflamed by a tremendous yearning.

—From a discourse of St. Bernard

Of all the saints, who enflames me the most with "a tremendous yearning" for the things of God? Why? How can I emulate him or her in one specific way today?

November 2

ALL SOULS

*Some souls would suffer in Purgatory until
the Day of Judgment if they were not relieved
by the prayers of the Church.*

—Traditionally attributed to St. Robert Bellarmine

What offering or sacrifice can I make today to benefit the holy souls in Purgatory?

November 3

ST. MARTIN DE PORRES,
RELIGIOUS (1579–1639)

---

*The virtuous example and even the conversation of this
saintly man exerted a powerful influence in drawing
men to religion. . . . If only everyone could learn this
lesson from the example that Martin gave us.*

—From a homily of Pope John XXIII at the
canonization of St. Martin de Porres

What do my example and my conversation with others
speak about me?

THE LIFE OF ST. MARTIN DE PORRES

Juan Martin de Porres Velazquez was the illegitimate son of a Spanish nobleman and a freed Panamanian slave. Born in Lima, Peru, in December 1579, he was a friend of Sts. Juan Macias and Rose of Lima; all three of them were affiliated with the Dominican Order.

Martin's father abandoned his mistress, Ana, after having a second child with her. The young boy ended up apprenticing with a barber and surgeon (the two professions were tightly linked at the time); his talent for healing was recognized early in his life. He was known to spend many hours in prayer, and he desired to enter religious life.

Peruvian law forbade those with African or native backgrounds from becoming full members of religious orders, so

Martin served as a servant first at the Dominican Holy Rosary Priory, then at the Convent of the Rosary, both in Lima. Over time he was given more responsibilities, and his holiness and commitment to charity were obvious. The prior was so impressed that he ignored the law and accepted Martin as a tertiary and then as a lay brother—a full member of the community who was not ordained a priest.

For much of the rest of his life, Br. Martin ran the priory infirmary. He would often bring the poor and the sick from the streets to the infirmary to care for them, and many miraculous healings were attributed to him. When a fellow brother criticized him for taking an ulcerous beggar into his own bed, Martin replied: "Compassion, my dear brother, is preferable to cleanliness."

St. Martin de Porres died on November 3, 1639, as one of the most beloved men in Peru. He is a patron of the poor and the oppressed.

November 4

ST. CHARLES BORROMEO,
BISHOP (1538–1584)

*My brothers, you must realize that for us churchmen
nothing is more necessary than meditation. We must
meditate before, during, and after everything we do. The
prophet says: "I will pray, and then I will understand."*

—From a homily of St. Charles Borromeo

What place in my prayer life does meditation on Sacred
Scripture or on the truths of the Faith hold? How has
it helped to understand God, myself, and others better?

November 5

*My vocation is to let myself be led like
a child, one day at a time.*

— Traditionally attributed to Blessed Pierina Morosini

To what extent do I let myself be led by God "like a child, one day at a time"? What characteristics do I have that help or hinder me in this pursuit?

November 6

Our God is God. All is as He pleases. I am the happiest creature in the thought that not the least thing can happen but by His will or permission; and all for the best.

—From the writings of St. Elizabeth Ann Seton

How can I apply the truth of this quote to a current struggle or difficulty? To what extent does this bring me a sense of peace?

November 7

---

*Untilled ground, however rich, will bring forth
thistles and thorns; so also the mind of man.*

—From the maxims of St. Teresa of Ávila

In what ways can I till the ground of my mind so that it will bring forth abundant fruit for the Kingdom of God? What resolution am I willing to make in this regard?

November 8

We must keep near to the souls God puts in our way, and try to understand and love them. Here we have discovered, by God's grace, the sources of peace and the means of possessing it fully.

— Servant of God Elisabeth Leseur,
The Secret Diary of Elisabeth Leseur

Who is one soul near to me whom I can "try to understand and love"? How can I reframe my perspective to see this individual as an instrument of God meant to lead me to true peace and virtue?

November 9

DEDICATION OF ST. JOHN LATERAN

When Christ came, He banished the devil from our hearts, in order to build in them a temple for Himself. Let us therefore do what we can with His help, so that our evil deeds will not deface the temple.

—From a homily of St. Caesarius of Arles

What stone of virtue can I use today to help build a temple for Christ within myself? What one defaced stone can I work to remove?

November 10

ST. LEO THE GREAT, POPE
AND DOCTOR (D. 461)

*The word made flesh lived among us, and in redeeming
the whole race, Christ gave himself entirely.*

—From a homily of St. Leo the Great

How do I see this definition of love as total self-donation
lived out in God the Father? In God the Son? In God
the Holy Spirit? In the Blessed Virgin Mary? In myself?

November 11

ST. MARTIN OF TOURS, BISHOP (316–397)

Death could not defeat him nor toil dismay him. He was quite without a preference of his own; he neither feared to die nor refused to live. With eyes and hands always raised to heaven, he never withdrew his unconquered spirit from prayer.

—From a letter of Sulpicius Severus on St. Martin of Tours

Which descriptions in this quotation describe me? Which do not?

November 12

ST. JOSAPHAT, BISHOP AND MARTYR (1580–1623)

[St. Josaphat] felt that God had inspired him to restore worldwide unity to the Church. Concerned mainly with seeing his own people reunited to the See of Peter, he sought every available argument that would foster and maintain Church unity.

—From a homily of Pope Pius XII (paraphrase)

Is God calling me to be a peacemaker and a unifier? How can I be a source of unity in my family? My friendships? My parish? My community?

November 13

ST. FRANCES XAVIER CABRINI, VIRGIN (1850–1917)

*O Jesus, I love you very much. Give me a heart
as big as the universe. Tell me what You wish
that I do, and do with me as You will.*

—Traditionally attributed to St. Frances Xavier Cabrini

St. Frances Cabrini's request of God shows her magnanimity. Magnanimity is a moral virtue closely related to fortitude. It means a person is noble of mind and heart; generous in forgiving; above revenge or resentment; unselfish and gracious. A magnanimous person is willing to take on great endeavors for the Kingdom of God. When have I displayed this virtue? Today, I will pray for more opportunities to exercise magnanimity.

November 14

---

*By reading and reflecting I found God; but by
praying I believed that God found me and that
He is a living reality and that we can love Him
in the same way that we can love a person.*

—From the writings of Servant of God Madeleine Delbrel

In this quote we hear about the difference between *knowing
about* God and *knowing* God. Which applies to me? What
does this indicate about my life of prayer?

November 15

ST. ALBERT THE GREAT, BISHOP AND DOCTOR (1206–1280)

[Jesus] could not have commanded anything more beneficial, for this sacrament is the fruit of the tree of life. Anyone who receives this sacrament with the devotion of sincere faith will never taste death.

—From a homily of St. Albert the Great on the Holy Eucharist

To what extent do I receive Holy Communion with sincere faith? Is there anything I can do to increase my devotion?

November 16

ST. GERTRUDE, VIRGIN (1256–1301)

*Eternal Father, I offer Thee the most precious blood of Thy
Divine Son, Jesus, in union with the Masses said throughout
the world today for all the holy souls in purgatory, for
sinners everywhere, for sinners in the universal church,
those in my own home, and within my family. Amen.*

—Prayer given to St. Gertrude by Jesus

Jesus promised that every time this prayer is said, a thousand
souls will be released from Purgatory and allowed into God's
presence. Am I willing to incorporate this prayer into my daily
life? I will show my sincerity of heart by praying it again right
now.

November 17

ST. ELIZABETH OF HUNGARY, RELIGIOUS (1207–1231)

I declare before God that I have seldom seen a more contemplative woman. When she was coming from private prayer, some religious men and women often saw her face shining marvelously and light coming from her eyes like the rays of the sun.

—From a letter of Conrad of Marburg, spiritual director of St. Elizabeth of Hungary

A nd we all, with unveiled face, beholding the glory of the Lord, are being changed into his likeness from one degree of glory to another; for this comes from the Lord who is the Spirit" (2 Corinthians 3:18). How does this passage explain the phenomena related in this quotation about St. Elizabeth? How does this encourage me?

THE LIFE OF ST. ELIZABETH OF HUNGARY

Elizabeth was born a princess of the Kingdom of Hungary in July 1207. In order to confirm an alliance, at the age of four she was sent to the court of Thuringia, in what is now east-central Germany, where she was slated to marry the eldest son of the ruler, Hermann. When Hermann died at a young age, Elizabeth's betrothal passed to the next son, Ludwig.

It is said that Elizabeth was a prayerful child and that her piety ruffled the feathers of Thuringia's extravagant courtiers. At the age of fourteen it was time for her to marry Ludwig, seven years her elder, who was a kind, doting, and protective husband. The couple had three children.

Ludwig now ruled Thuringia, and in his brief reign he and Elizabeth were well loved by their people. Despite her station,

Elizabeth performed personal acts of charity for the poor; she also used her station to organize widespread giving to the poor, including from the personal goods and fortunes of the royal family. In all these activities Ludwig supported her.

In 1227, when Elizabeth was just twenty, Ludwig died from illness while on a crusade. Elizabeth was devastated. She was forced out of Thuringia and had to fight for her dowry, but when she finally received it, she gave much to the poor and used the rest to build a hospital in which she personally served.

It is said that in 1228 she became one of the very first Franciscan tertiaries in Germany, and to this day she is considered a patron of the Third Order of St. Francis. St. Elizabeth of Hungary died in 1231 at the age of twenty-four.

November 18

Whenever any grievous temptation or vehement sorrow oppresses thee, invoke thy guardian, thy leader; cry out to him and say, "Lord, save us, lest we perish!"

—St. Bernard, recorded in *Lives of the Saints* by Fr. Alban Butler

---

Is there a "grievous temptation" or a "vehement sorrow" that is oppressing me today? Am I willing to take it to the Sacrament of Reconciliation and seek the grace of the Lord?

November 19

Faith is a gift, but for very few is it a gift given without any demand for equal time devoted to its cultivation.

—From a letter of Flannery O'Connor

In what ways do I devote time to the cultivation of a mature Catholic faith?

November 20

I have given everything to my Master: He will take care of me. The best thing for us is not what we consider best, but what the Lord wants for us.

—Traditionally attributed to St. Josephine Bakhita

Is there something that I am holding on to that I am afraid to surrender? What is it? Can I trust God to do what is best? Now, in confidence, I will release this concern to Him.

November 21

PRESENTATION OF THE BLESSED VIRGIN MARY

Mary is the heart of the Church. This is why all works of charity spring from her. It is well known that the heart has two movements: systole and diastole. Thus Mary is always performing these two movements: absorbing grace from her Most Holy Son, and pouring it forth on sinners.

—Traditionally attributed to St. Anthony Mary Claret

As a child of Mary, how can I imitate her as "the heart of the Church"? In what ways can I live this out daily?

November 22

FEAST OF ST. CECILIA, VIRGIN AND MARTYR (SECOND CENTURY)

*"Rejoice in the L*ORD*, O you righteous!*
Praise befits the upright.
*Praise the L*ORD *with the lyre,*
Make melody to him with the harp of ten strings!
Sing to him a new song,
Play skillfully on the strings, with loud shouts."

—Psalm 33:1–3

What is my song of praise to the Lord today?

November 23

FEAST OF ST. COLUMBAN, ABBOT (D. 615)

* * *

If man applies the virtues planted in his soul to the right purpose, he will be like God. The image we depict must not be that of one who is unlike God; for one who is harsh and irascible and proud would display the image of a despot. Let us not imprint on ourselves the image of a despot, but let Christ paint his image in us.

—From an instruction of St. Columban

* * *

Which virtues are the opposites of harshness, irascibility, and pride? How can I employ these virtues today to be more like God?

November 24

FEAST OF ANDREW DUNG-LAC, PRIEST, AND COMPANIONS, MARTYRS (NINETEENTH CENTURY)

In the midst of these torments, which usually terrify others, I am, by the grace of God, full of joy and gladness, because I am not alone—Christ is with me.

—From a letter of St. Paul Le-Bao-Tinh
contemplating his impending martyrdom

Hidden in the words of this passage is the great truth of the grace of martyrdom. How does this quell any fears that I might have in my life? Have I experienced a similar grace when I have been under fire for the Faith? How does this increase my confidence in God?

November 25

FEAST OF ST. CATHERINE OF ALEXANDRIA (CA. 287–CA. 305)

"Before she was poor, and now she is rich; before she was ignorant, and now she is truly wise; before she was proud, and now she is humble. She is now worthy and I accept her as my bride."

—Jesus to His Mother about St. Catherine of Alexandria, given to the saint in a dream following her baptism (traditional)

Of the graces of baptism, which do I most need to experience right now?

November 26

Our Lord who saved the world through the Cross will only work for the good of souls through the Cross.

—Traditionally attributed to St. Madeleine Sophie Barat

What cross am I currently carrying? In what way is God working through it for the good of my soul and the souls of others?

November 27

The duty of the moment is what you should be doing at any given time, in whatever place God has put you. Your doing the duty of the moment, your living the nitty gritty, daily routine of ordinary life, can uncover the face of Christ in the marketplace . . . where you work or play or eat . . . or wherever.

—Catherine de Hueck Doherty, *Dear Parents*

What is my duty of the moment right now? How is Christ presenting His face to me? I will consciously seek Him through every duty and moment of my day today.

GOD IS ALWAYS
SPEAKING TO US

God is always about the business of revealing His will to us. He is always speaking to us. All we need to do is have ears to hear. During a recent radio broadcast, I read a passage from St. Teresa of Ávila that included this teaching: "I would recommend to anyone to whom a good inspiration repeatedly comes, never to neglect it out of fear. If he turns nakedly to God alone, he need not be afraid of failure, since God is all powerful."

These words are important because they help us avert one of Satan's greatest tactics. He provokes fear in our hearts in order to prevent us from moving forward in a work to which God has called us. Often, this is a fear of failure.

That day, multiple people contacted the show by phone and e-mail to say that this teaching from St. Teresa helped them work through difficult decisions by reminding them to trust in the Lord. Through St. Teresa and our little program, God had spoken to them.

God is always speaking to us. He talks to us through prayer, through Sacred Scripture, through the lives of the saints, and through each other. And yes, He speaks to us through television programs, radio programs, social media, and so on.

Our God is a God of revelation, and even now He is revealing Himself to us. Do we hear Him? Are we willing to say yes to Him? Let's place all of our trust in His power and might. God alone will see us through.

November 28

Be of good cheer, only work, only strive cheerfully; for nothing is lost. Every prayer of yours, every psalm you sing is recorded. Every alms, every fast is recorded.

—St. Cyril of Jerusalem, *Catechetical Lectures*

How can I show good cheer during this dark time of the year? What can I offer up to the Lord this Advent season?

November 29

I guess that is what dying must be like; to be finished and to be able to look back at the struggles of life, and know that God was your constant companion.

—Mother Angelica, from her television program

How has God been my companion through the struggles of my life? I will pray for the spiritual eyes to see this reality.

November 30

FEAST OF ST. ANDREW, APOSTLE

As he walked by the Sea of Galilee, he saw two brothers,
Simon who is called Peter and Andrew his brother,
casting a net into the sea. . . . And he said to them,
"Follow me, and I will make you fishers of men."
Immediately they left their nets and followed him.

—Matthew 4:18, 19–20

Through our baptism, Jesus has called each one of us to be "fishers of men." How do I think of this reality in reference to myself? What is my current sea of evangelization? What nets may I need to leave behind so I can fish in it?

Chapter Twelve

Meditations

FOR

DECEMBER

December 1

Many who confess their venial sins out of custom and concern for order but without thought of amendment remain burdened with them for their whole life and thus lose many spiritual benefits and advantages.

—St. Francis de Sales, *Introduction to the Devout Life*

What sins in my life, if any, do I seem to confess over and over again? How am I actively seeking to amend them and overcome them?

December 2

How often have I thought that I may owe all the graces I've received to the prayers of a person who begged them from God for me, and whom I shall know only in heaven.

—St. Thérèse of Lisieux, *Story of a Soul*

For whom am I secretly praying today?

December 3

FEAST OF ST. FRANCIS XAVIER, PRIEST (1506–1552)

Many, many people hereabouts are not becoming Christians for one reason only: there is nobody to make them Christians.

—From a letter of St. Francis Xavier to St. Ignatius Loyola

In what practical ways can I help to "make" people Christians in the midst of my everyday witness to the Faith?

December 4

ST. DAMASCENE, PRIEST AND DOCTOR OF THE CHURCH (D. 749)

What then, is more precious than to be in the hand of God? For God is Life and Light, and those who are in God's hand are in life and light.

—St. John Damascene, *Exposition of the Orthodox Faith*

If I am in the state of grace (having no mortal sin on my soul), then I am in God's hand. Therefore, according to St. John of Damascus, I am "in life and light." Today, I will consciously seek to see the life and the light in my everyday duties and responsibilities, and I will thank God for them in my time of prayer tonight.

December 5

I am a crooked piece of iron and am come into religion to be made straight by the hammer of mortification and penance.

—Traditionally attributed to St. Aloysius Gonzaga

What is my "hammer" today? How can I use it to prepare me for the coming of the Lord?

December 6

FEAST OF ST. NICHOLAS, BISHOP
(D. THIRD CENTURY)

He was exceedingly well brought up by his parents
and trod piously in their footsteps. The child, watched
over by the Church, enlightened his mind and
encouraged his thirst for sincere and true religion.

—From an early Life of St. Nicholas

Dear St. Nicholas, on this your feast day, obtain for me the grace to enlighten my mind and encourage my thirst for sincerity and truth given to me through the teachings of our Holy Catholic Church. Pray for me that I may have wisdom in understanding and true discernment regarding the life of faith. Help me to rid myself of false perceptions, heretical concepts, and erroneous teachings that can lead me away from truth. Thank you for your prayers for me this day. Amen.

December 7

ST. AMBROSE, BISHOP AND DOCTOR OF THE CHURCH (340–397)

The star of morn to night succeeds;
We therefore meekly pray,
May God in all our words and deeds,
Keep us from harm this day;
May He in love restrain us still
From tones of strife and words of ill,
And wrap around and close our eyes
To earth's absorbing vanities.
Amen.

—A morning hymn attributed to St. Ambrose
and translated by Bl. John Henry Newman

In what four specific ways does St. Ambrose ask God to protect us from harm this day? What can I do specifically to cooperate with the protective grace God will give me?

THE LIFE OF ST. AMBROSE

Ambrose was born into a patrician family in mid-fourth-century Milan. He quickly rose in the ranks of the civil authorities; by 372, in his early thirties, he was governor of one of the most important provinces in the Roman Empire.

He was so popular that, although he wasn't even baptized, the people clamored for him to be named Bishop of Milan upon the previous bishop's death in 374. He fled the exuberant mob, but a letter from the emperor compelled him to accept the position; he was baptized, ordained, and consecrated as bishop. Two famous stories illustrate how he grew into his new role.

Ambrose was elevated to this role at a difficult time for the Church as the Arian heresy was strong throughout Europe. By the mid-380s, even the Roman emperor (in Constantinople) and his wife were Arians. They demanded that two churches in Milan be handed over to the Arian heretics, but Ambrose personally stayed in one of the churches with the faithful until the Arians relented. It is said by some that the prayers they sang in that church were the inspiration for the Liturgy of the Hours.

But the most famous story about Ambrose is his reaction to Emperor Theodosius's massacre in Thessalonica. The bishop refused to administer the sacraments to the emperor until he confessed and did public penance for his brutal sin. Theodosius submitted to Ambrose, publicly prostrating himself in a Milanese church.

In addition to these exploits, Ambrose wrote many theological treatises; he is considered one of the Doctors of the Church. He also baptized another Doctor of the Church: St. Augustine. After twenty-three years of exemplary service to the Church, St. Ambrose of Milan died on April 4, 397.

December 8

IMMACULATE CONCEPTION OF THE BLESSED VIRGIN MARY

"Pure as the snow," we say. Ah! never flake
Fell through the air
One-tenth as fair
As Mary's soul was made for Christ's dear sake.
Virgin Immaculate,
The whitest whiteness of the Alpine snows,
Beside thy stainless spirit, dusky grows.

"Pure as the stars." Ah! never lovely night
Wore in its diadem
So pure a gem
As that which fills the ages with its light.
Virgin Immaculate,
The peerless splendors of thy soul by far
Outshine the glow of heaven's serenest star.

—"Mary Immaculate," Eleanor C. Donnelly

Dear Mother, You were kept free from the stain of original sin so that the Word of God could make His abode in You. Today, on this feast that celebrates Your Immaculate Conception, I ask You to obtain for me the grace I need to resist sin and to live for Christ alone. Be the mother of my soul. Nurture me in Your tender heart. Take my hand and lead me to Your Son. Amen.

December 9

ST. JUAN DIEGO (1474–1548)

I am a nobody, I am a small rope,
a tiny ladder, the tail end, a leaf.

—St. Juan Diego to the Our Lady of Guadalupe

St. Juan Diego, who describes himself as a "nobody," a "small rope," a "tiny ladder," the "tail end," a "leaf," was the instrument Our Lady of Guadalupe chose to join her in one of the greatest moments in evangelization. How do I describe myself? Am I too big to work with Our Lady? How can I exercise the virtue of humility to become smaller?

December 10

*The humble man is not cast down by the censures
or the slights of others. If he has unconsciously
given occasion for them, he amends the faults; if he
deserves them not, he treats them as trifles.*

—From a syndicated column of Ven. Fulton J. Sheen

How do I handle "the censures or slights of others"? What does Archbishop Sheen recommend when these situations occur? How will this help me grow in humility?

December 11

Humility in relation to love means thinking others better than ourselves. One advantage of this is that it gives us some examples to imitate. Pride, on the other hand, sometimes seeks first place that others may say, "Oh! What greatness!" Pride, too, can subtly take the last place that others may say, "What humility!"

—Ven. Fulton J. Sheen, from his *Life Is Worth Living* television program

Based on the quote above, what is one advantage to thinking better of others than of ourselves? Whom can I imitate? What are the two faces of pride exposed in the quote above? To what extent do I operate in either of these ways?

December 12

OUR LADY OF GUADALUPE

*I vividly desire that a church be built on this site,
so that in it I can be present and give my love,
compassion, help, and defense, for I am your most
devoted mother . . . to hear your laments and to
remedy all your miseries, pains, and sufferings.*

—The Blessed Mother to St. Juan Diego

Mary says she is my "most devoted mother." What does this mean, and what does it mean specifically to me? What lament do I currently want her to hear? What misery, pain, or suffering do I long for her to remedy? I will compose a short prayer to her now asking her to tuck all of this into her Immaculate Heart.

December 13

ST. LUCY, VIRGIN AND MARTYR (283–304)

The Word of God moves swiftly; He is not won by the lukewarm, nor held fast by the negligent. Let your soul be attentive to His word; follow carefully the path God tells you to take, for He is swift in His passing.

—St. Ambrose, *On Virginity*

The path to which God called St. Lucy led her to the crown of martyrdom. What path is God calling me to walk? Is there anything impeding my progress on it—lukewarmness or negligence? St. Lucy, pray for me that I might see clearly and move swiftly to fulfill God's most holy will. Amen.

December 14

ST. JOHN OF THE CROSS, PRIEST AND DOCTOR OF THE CHURCH (1542–1591)

Would that men might come at last to see that it is quite impossible to reach the thicket of the riches and wisdom of God except by first entering the thicket of much suffering, in such a way that the soul finds there its consolation and desire. The soul that longs for divine wisdom chooses first, and in truth, to enter the thicket of the Cross.

—St. John of the Cross, *Spiritual Canticle*

How does St. John's statement contrast with worldly wisdom? What is my attitude toward the crosses in my life? Can I adjust my perspective and see the great treasure hidden in the suffering and trial?

December 15

Observe that we gain more in a single day by trials which come to us from God and our neighbor than we would in ten years by penances and other exercises, which we take up of ourselves.

—St. Teresa of Ávila, *The Interior Castle*

How can the above quotation of St. Teresa of Ávila help me to see the great treasure hidden in the contradictions and sufferings of daily life?

December 16

There are three distinct comings of the Lord of which I know: His coming to men, His coming into men, and His coming against men.

—From a homily of St. Bernard

How have I experienced all three of these comings of Jesus in my life? What is my response to God about these visitations?

December 17

Pray. Pray and sacrifice yourselves for sinners,
for many souls go to hell because they have
no one to sacrifice or pray for them.

—Our Lady of Fátima

How am I heeding these words of Our Blessed Lady?

December 18

Like the dawning of the morning,
On the mountain's golden heights,
Like the breaking of the moonbeams
On the gloom of cloudy nights.
Like a secret told by angels,
Getting known upon the earth,
Is the Mother's expectation
Of Messias' speedy birth.

—Fr. Frederick William Faber

What is my expectation for this Christmas time? How can I unite myself to Our Lady in this regard?

AND A CHILD SHALL
LEAD THEM

One of the great blessings in my life is being a grandparent. My grandchildren teach me so much. Take Carmen, for example. When she became a big sister to her younger brother, I began to see so many beautiful qualities develop in her. She treated him with patience, kindness, and thoughtfulness. Much to his delight, she gleefully rushed to him when she returned from school. She played with him, doted on him, and told everyone she met that he was her baby brother.

I can remember wondering how Carmen would handle her brother's arrival. She had been an only child for five years and was very accustomed to having her parents' full attention. But the new arrival enriched her and enhanced her lovely feminine graces.

Change can do that. It holds the possibility for us to expand as persons and to grow in virtue. Change can help us discover character strengths we never knew we had and bring to the surface latent talents and gifts. It really depends on gratitude for that which God is entrusting to us, and an openness of heart to explore the opportunities change may hold.

I don't think Carmen thought about any of these things when she became a big sister. With childlike simplicity, she simply embraced the idea.

This has taught me a lot and encouraged personal reflection. To what extent do I embrace change with gratitude and openness of heart? I know one thing—I will be thinking of Carmen the next time change comes my way.

December 19

Prepare the way of the Lord, make his paths straight.

—Matthew 3:3

In what one way today can I prepare the way of the Lord?

December 20

It is full time now for you to wake from sleep. For salvation is nearer to us now than when we first believed; the night is far gone, the day is at hand. Let us then cast off the works of darkness and put on the armor of light.

—Romans 13:11–12

To prepare for the Savior's birth, what one deed of darkness must I cast off, and what one piece of armor must I put on in its place?

December 21

FEAST OF ST. PETER CANISIUS, PRIEST AND DOCTOR OF THE CHURCH (1521–1597)

So, after daring to approach your most loving heart and to plunge my thirst in it, I received a promise from you of a garment made of three parts: these were to cover my soul in its nakedness, and to belong especially to my religious profession. They were peace, love and perseverance. Protected by this garment of salvation, I was confident that I would lack nothing but all would succeed and give you glory.

—From the writings of St. Peter Canisius

In preparation for the birth of Jesus, which part of the "garment of salvation" do I most need to put on? In what one way can I utilize it today?

December 22

We should go to prayer with deep humility and an awareness of our nothingness. We must invoke the help of the Holy Spirit and that of our good angel, and then remain still during this time in God's presence, full of faith that He is more in us than we are in ourselves.

—from an instruction of St. Jane Frances de Chantal to her Sisters of the Visitation

As I continue to seek the virtue of humility in preparation to receive the Christ Child in the womb of my heart, what advice does St. Jane de Chantal give me? How can I act on it today?

December 23

ST. JOHN OF KANTY, PRIEST (1390–1473)

*With his humility went a rare and childlike simplicity . . .
the thoughts of his heart were revealed in his words and
actions. If he suspected that someone had taken offense at
speaking the truth, before going to the altar he would ask
forgiveness for what was not so much his own sin as the
other person's misunderstanding. . . . The God in his heart
and the God on his lips were one and the same God.*

—From a letter of Pope Clement XIII on St. John of Kanty

What about St. John's example speaks to me the most?
How do I wish to respond?

December 24

O come, O come, Emmanuel,
And ransom captive Israel,
That mourns in lonely exile here,
Until the Son of God appear.
Rejoice! rejoice! Emmanuel
Shall come to thee, O Israel.

—"Veni, Veni Emmanuel"

What place of "exile" within myself most needs to experience the Savior's presence? Today, I will offer this part of myself to Him as an act of love and humility.

December 25

NATIVITY OF THE LORD

Hark! A glad exulting throng;
Hark! The loud hosannas ring;
Glad hosannas loud and long
Greet Messiah triumphing.

He, of Whom the prophets won
Mystic visions faint and dim,
Comes, the All-Father's only Son,
And redemption comes with Him.

— "Christi Caterva Clamitat"

W hat is my personal hymn of praise on this day of my Savior's birth? I will sing it now to my Lord and my Savior!

December 26

ST. STEPHEN, FIRST MARTYR

My brothers, Christ made love the stairway that would enable all Christians to climb to heaven. Hold fast to it, therefore, in all sincerity, give one another practical proof of it, and by your progress in it, make your ascent together.

—From a homily of St. Fulgentius of Ruspe
on the Feast of St. Stephen

What practical proof of love can I give today?

December 27

ST. JOHN, APOSTLE AND EVANGELIST

Beloved, let us love one another; for love is of God, and he who loves is born of God and knows God. He who does not love does not know God; for God is love. In this the love of God was made manifest among us, that God sent his only Son into the world, so that we might live through him. In this is love, not that we loved God but that he loved us and sent his Son to be the expiation for our sins. Beloved, if God so loved us, we also ought to love one another.

1 John 4:7–11

According to St. John's definition of love, to what extent am I a loving person? How can loving God more and receiving more of His love help me to increase my ability to love others?

December 28

HOLY INNOCENTS, MARTYRS

How great a gift of grace is here! To what merits of their own do the children owe this kind of victory? They cannot speak, yet they bear witness to Christ. They cannot use their limbs to engage in battle, yet already they bear off the palm of victory.

—From a homily of St. Quodvultdeus on the Holy Innocents

How do I bear witness to Christ in my words and in my deeds? Am I willing to bear witness through the gift of my life? Why or why not?

December 29

ST. THOMAS BECKET, BISHOP AND MARTYR (CA. 1119–1170)

The whole company of saints bears witness to the unfailing truth that without real effort no one wins the crown.

—From a letter of St. Thomas Becket

Sanctity comes with effort. What effort am I making on a daily basis to attain holiness of life?

December 30

Without the Way, there is no going; without the Truth, there is no knowing; without the Life there is no living.

—St. Thomas à Kempis, *The Imitation of Christ*

As this year comes to a close, in what specific way does this quote help me to formulate a spiritual plan for the new year? How can I enter more deeply into the Way to know where I am going, into the Truth to learn what I should know, and into the Life so that I may truly live?

THE LIFE OF ST. THOMAS BECKET

Thomas Becket was born into a noble family in London in 1119 or 1120. He was well educated and rose quickly in law positions within the Church structure, especially at the important Archdiocese of Canterbury. His work was so well-regarded that in 1155 he was appointed Lord Chancellor by King Henry II—the same position that would be held by St. Thomas More under Henry VIII centuries later.

As Lord Chancellor, Becket had a strong relationship with the king, even fostering the king's son in his home, as was customary at the time. The civil servant also collected tax income for the crown, even from the Church.

Seven years into his service, Becket was nominated to be the next Archbishop of Canterbury. He was ordained and consecrated, and King Henry figured he had his man in the cathedral. He was wrong.

Rather than acquiescing to the growing claims of sovereignty of the crown over the Church, Archbishop Becket pushed back, asserting the independence of the Church from royal control. Henry responded by pressing the Constitutions of Clarendon, which accentuated the rights of the king over church matters. Becket was the only English bishop who refused to sign, and he was exiled to France.

Rome attempted to broker a peace between Becket and Henry, and in 1170 the archbishop was able to return to Canterbury. But Becket continued to press his claims against the crown. It has been passed down that, in the presence of his court, Henry exclaimed, "Who will rid me of this troublesome priest?"

Some of Henry's knights took this rhetorical question as an order, and they marched to Canterbury and killed the archbishop in his cathedral on December 29, 1170. The location of St. Thomas Becket's martyrdom is marked and venerated to this day.

December 31

ST. SYLVESTER, POPE (D. 335)

*I have fought the good fight, I have finished the race, I
have kept the faith. Henceforth there is laid up for me
the crown of righteousness, which the Lord, the righteous
judge, will award to me on that Day, and not only to
me but also to all who have loved his appearing.*

2 Timothy 4:7–8

Dear St. Sylvester, You were the Vicar of Christ when the
Arian heresy and the Donatist schism caused great
discord and division within the Church. How often you must
have felt the pain and suffering of the body of Christ! But,
instead of losing courage, you persevered and the Church
came through this difficult time. Today, I ask for your intercession. Obtain for me the grace I need to remain steadfast

in adversity, courageous in contradiction, and persevering in trial. Thank you for your prayers and supplications on my behalf. Amen.

About the Author

Johnnette S. Benkovic is the founder and president of Living His Life Abundantly® and Women of Grace®, a Catholic apostolate to women, whose mission is to transform the world one woman at a time through a program of spiritual formation. She is host of the international EWTN weekday television and radio programs *Women of Grace* and *Women of Grace Live*. A sought-after speaker, Johnnette presents on a variety of topics in various settings and geographic locations.

She is also founder and president of the Benedicta Leadership Institute for Women®, whose mission is to identify, educate, develop, and train Catholic women to be active leaders and mentors of the day in accord with their state in life. She has developed both a certification program and a Masters of Theology program in Catholic Women's Leadership in partnership with SS. Cyril and Methodius Seminary in Orchard Lake, Michigan.

A mother and grandmother, Johnnette was married for thirty-three years until the death of her husband. She is the author of several books and has developed study programs for women and teenage girls. For more information on her writings as well as the outreaches of Women of Grace®, visit www.womenofgrace.com.